T0064014

AGE OF Discovery

Early Life and Times of Robin Blessed - Part Two

ROBIN P. BLESSED

PARTRIDGE

A Penguin Random House Company

To order additional copies of this book, contact
Toll Free 800 101 2657 (Singapore)
Toll Free 1 800 81 7340 (Malaysia)
orders.singapore@partridgepublishing.com

www.partridgepublishing.com/singapore

Dedicated to All Readers
Blessed are those who have read the first book,
'Age of Innocence' and will read this second one,
'Age of Discovery'

CONTENTS

WHAT READERS SAY . . . ABOUT THE BOOK: 'AGE OF INNOCENCE'

———◆◇◆———

I have enjoyed your book tremendously. It had helped me to begin to appreciate the events in my own life. It is a book with deep and meaningful thoughts . . . a very unique book.

—*Wu Wanjin*, Educator.

God's hand is in all that happens and the book reminds us how His righteousness prevails. Robin is able to relay his story without hints of bitterness or anger, of haughtiness or pride. The writing style is direct, concise, clear, and relevant . . . without attempts to overdrive emotions yet with just the right precision to describe the intention . . . and space enough for those moments to hold back lumps in the throat.

The writing approach is uncommon in that Robin shows even as a 'natural' man he had yearned and search for his beginnings. Now, spiritually enlightened he is able to see that God was there all the time guiding the way . . . throughout his early life, and at the end it marvels me that the Lord Jesus stands glorified still in all the years that Robin had ignored Him. I hope for more of such biographies to become useful as tools to bring out the goodness of our Lord both to unbelievers and to fellow believers.

—*Cedric Tan*, Parent, Manager.

The book brought back many fond memories of my life at the age of innocence. Truly, "to everything there is a season, and a time to every purpose under the heaven". God makes each of us different and gives us just as varied experiences in life with people, incidents, and things around us; though we may not acknowledge God's existence then.

All things that happened in life, for good or bad, joyous or sorrowful, all were just transient and eventually came to pass and became part of our memory to be aware and by reflecting, to improve and consciously change what we can. Without awareness we are overwhelmed, drowned in self-pity and be unfruitful. Since knowing Christ, memories and reflection redirected my spirit to that of thanksgiving, of thankfulness, of gratitude to God for His longsuffering, goodness, grace and mercy upon even one lost soul such as me.

The author has likewise put together pieces of fond memories in his early life for a purpose: in praise and thanksgiving to the Creator, Saviour, and Lord in his life, and through sharing it that many may come to know this great love of God. *For all this I considered in my heart even to declare all this that the righteous, and the wise, and their works, are in the hand of God: no man knoweth either love or hatred by all that is before them.*—Ecclesiastes 9:1. May the glory and love of God shine upon the heart of every reader and be blessed.

—*Samantha Quau*, Parent, Homemaker, Home-school Educator.

An interesting book to read . . . In its use of simple flashback in time, many fond nostalgic familiar glimpses of my own journey during the age of innocence came to the fore for reflection. Throughout, the book highlights the importance of acknowledging God and having a personal relationship with Him, who is the very centre of our lives.

—*S.M. Vijayaratnam*, Parent, Senior Manager.

I enjoyed the Age of Innocence very much. I appreciate the author's reflections of his childhood—the past is not simply a distant collective memory of irreversible events, happenings and acts (and perhaps, omissions). A careful examination of childhood has shown the imprint of God's presence and provision. The past has its purpose, a purpose rooted in the source of the purpose who is the giver of life. I find myself reminded of a line in Shakespeare's *The Tempest*—"What's past is Prologue". Indeed, the past has, and will have, an undeniable role in the making of our current present and our future. God is the master weaver, and what an amazing tapestry we will see in the life of the author. This book faithfully reproduces the author's discovery of God's blessings throughout the earliest years of his life. Truly, God loads us with benefits, daily, from our beginning. Childhood can be full of richness. I am inspired. And I look forward to the Prologue that is to come.

—*April Mak*, Solicitor.

It is a book worthy of an afternoon curled up on the couch to look back in time: to reflect on what God and our parents have done for us, at the same time to count our many blessings.

—*Zhang Meifen,* Medical Practitioner.

INTRODUCTION

Truth, common truth is what an author can ascribe to himself. That truth as beholden and drawn from his life experiences, presented simply with diligence and accuracy, is without varnish or embellishment. In and through these shared experiences that you the reader may hear the author's voice. Experiences alone can mean little. All of us have them. Like jigsaw pieces how do they bring to life the tapestry of meaningful congruence, not so much in trying to jig-fit them but rather to let them tell the story. It is unlike a collage of colours or patchwork on a canvas to create some vague whimsical fleeting sense of beauty, ecstasy, and 'life' out of lifelessness and impermanence, where images form by chance and receive creative aesthetic acclaim. It is not about techniques alone. It is expression of the painter's experience unique to him, deeply felt by him, truth as he sees it. He translates it through techniques that best illustrate the intensity of his experience. Experiences must go through the 'fining' pot of reflection, of contemplation to reveal and manifest their place in time, their purpose. They exist here in our lives on this earth characterised by the temporal, the transient, and must not serve ends that terminate with our earthly existence and demise *per se*, from dust to dust: that would be certain tragedy.

Our experiences must give us meaning, must translate to an eternal purpose that transcends impermanence to perfection. While we breathe and walk this earth, we can make that happen only with reflection seeking to understand how they make sense in the greater and eternal scheme of life . . . *continually seeking the truth*. A recapitulation of the age of innocence appropriately bridges it to the age of discovery, bringing to bear the contrasts, differences, shifts, transitions, and variations, humanly classed as *change*. This in turn aids an understanding of the author's frame of reference, bearings, position, and condition in relation to change. Then only can the reader address and apprehend the author's emotional and mental states between the *ages*.

Age of Innocence: A Recapitulation

In the first book, *Age of Innocence,* the author shared events and experiences entering upon his life between ages 3 and 12. There was no roller coaster, just a happy low hum, with little variableness during the Age of Innocence, it was always up, always looking for more, never bothered about adversity, every moment to live and enjoy in, with an air of positive expectancy. He wanted to do everything, experience everything, to see everything, to learn everything, to know everything. The passion for them is intense as though that was what living was about. It was simply a time of youthful generous enthusiasm with a childlike disregard for the world's judgement. There was no heavy baggage to lift, no toiling burdens to interfere with the pleasure of the moment, no difficult past to haunt, and no visible future with which to contend. We said '*life is not a little bundle of big things; it is a big bundle of little things*'. These little things were small in space and short in time. They were really a big bundle of little '*light*' things. They were pleasurable, memorable experiences, light and simple, for the learning, and becoming a part of our persona . . . perhaps to brace us for the future 'ages'.

Age of Discovery: Age 13 to 16

This book is a continuation of the age of innocence with changing shades as life hits a different terrain where dust clouds obscure the view, the space around barren and dreary, prospects uncertain, while gloomy clouds descend. It is an uncanny scene, unsettling and strange, difficult to keep a hold on the handle, a little slippery, and it takes a while longer to get on the tracks and be on the ascendant. Certain trepidation had found its way into the uncertainty of expectations. Tentativeness offered discomfort as in driving along a contoured upward sloping road with no markers or signs in sight—one cannot see ahead nor discern comfortably until one is there just beyond the hump—with the imagined probability of driving past the hump and over a cliff at the next squeeze of the pedal—to go or not to go. There is a certain taunting precipitated by real and imagined limitations. Even in the real limitations, it is between the worth of the effort and the risk. With the imagined, there is a tug between what is and that perceived; the former cannot be weighed, and the latter quite measureless. There was even a seeming subjectivity to the notion of relativity, a moving target of sort. What was simple in the age of innocence had become a little bit complex. Indecision has crept into contention like coarse grit in our canvas shoes irritating our feet with every step we take: moving presses against and hurts, not moving irks the spirit and discomforts. Wherefore, the root of the problem remains unattended. The 'everything' he wants to do, to feel, to see, to learn, to tame, to conquer is not to happen: conflicts and contentions are in the way. The author has trouble manoeuvring along the unfamiliar route. With each difficulty the confidence erodes, uncertainty notches up until after a long delay he sees a spark of hope that keeps up the spirit to persevere and continue the journey regardless of the trouble. It seems a laborious stoicism. The journey has many travellers but bears an incomprehensible loneliness; there is a disconsolate lack of kindred companionship, friendless.

As someone set apart, travelling alone in desolation, he is without comfort, distanced from any oasis of solace, far from the familiar.

The arena has not changed for the author as he plays out life in the school and at home, his primary occupations; now, more so at school in the new environment. There is a need to make sense of and to adapt to longer hours in learning, a deluge of new knowledge, and a compression in the learning process; the commitment in extra-curricular activities, and the long travel to school and back home. The influence of school assumes a predominant place in the author's life as he becomes embroiled with all its nuances. Even when he is at home, there is homework to contend with, assignments to complete, helping siblings with their schoolwork; thinking and understanding required time and effort. The *reactive* innocence he knows from experience and is familiar with now takes on *intuitive* discovery, a new perceptive way to look at things; is untaught, is non-inferential. Pa and Mie (dad and mum) are completely befuddled in the transition; see the change in their son, and as helpless bystanders hope for the best of something far beyond their comprehension. They only watch with abandonment and attempts the occasional encouragement. They too, seem to be in their own age of discovery. Connection is naturally broken in overwhelming change where the gulf between the immediate generations grows uncontrollably wider from a perception bred in the cognitive process and inward exploration. Life is withdrawn and lonely. The author has no one older and wiser to direct or alleviate his loneliness. He has to go it alone. Hope lies only in pressing on stoically, laboriously, and is toilsome.

Life is as a race, the competitor pool is huge, more than twice what it used to be; the competitors are the best of the nation. Tall and short, fat and thin, light and dark, rich and poor, loud and quiet, strong and weak, they are all in this one pool. They will all run the *same* race. The hurdles are so much the higher, the obstacles more insidious, but they are the *same* for all. You start at the *same* point, where and when you end may be different, according to what you put into the race and your preparation. They call this *meritocracy*, a system where deserving advancement is on the merit of a measured attainment of excellence. Meritocracy is not new in the age of innocence where it also operated . . . what is different? Meritocracy in the age of discovery is about merit, deservingness, and the need to advance. There is an end, an end determined by an institutionalised system and implemented globally, and finally accepted almost globally. As in universal suffrage, the majority assents to it, consensus gathers around it, the law institutionalises it, and it becomes the accepted norm as opposition falls by the wayside, left on the fringes. Meritocracy rewards when one attains the ends, the goals of the system. It does not consider handicappers. We now grow up in it, take it in stride as a given, embrace it, and walk in it; choice and the freedom of it is outside the mainstream, is orthodox except for those who have access to the means. On the contrary, in the age of innocence, we do not think of the ends even though they are there, we think of relishing the moment, gratifying the curiosity, soaking in the wonderment. The means is also the end. The end is in the thing itself, the end is itself. Now, the little things have become bigger, and the 'lightness' has gathered some weight. The joy associated with the moment has now begun to wear off somewhat, that which came from within us now turns to the outside of us to consider the standards set and with approbation from the system. We are a part of this world. Do we even own enough of it to truly say we are a part of it, when we have to contend for it? We are imperfect as the world is imperfect, impermanent as it also is. There has to be a perfect world where contention does not come into play, where meritocracy has no basis to subsist, where we truly can enjoy our part in it, our place therein.

This second book attempts to cast experiences as strips of moving *scenes*—larger, broader than *events*—between ages 13 and 16 in the author's life, as shifting scenes to moderate a halting sense of his early life and times. The daily throb of life, of natural life is there but it does not quietly continue; there is a yearning wistful spirit that silently cries out for a seat in his heart. The seed has its root in nature; we have ours in things intangible, spiritual, in our source, our very beginnings . . . in our Creator. Our heart yearns to reconcile to that eternal Spirit but the impermanent world draws us to itself away from our roots. The author intends to discover how over time we become less of who we are; we become more of the world we live in, pressed on all sides to conform to the accepted norm. How far do we go? Is fitting in the only way to survive . . . ? Does survival underwrite us for the eternal purpose? Is survival then the end goal? Until we are drawn to and live in the spirit of our Creator, we are bound to the laws of nature. The laws of nature inform that man raised in dust, will likewise succumb to the dust. What then lives beyond the dust? We yearn for a world where there is no basis for 'survival of the fittest', for the idea of it is detestable; it compares with uncertainty and is questionable. In the world we yearn to be, all are 'fit' for it; that is all that matters; one has to be fit to be there. The sifting begins here in this present world where only one immutable unquestionable universal common basis qualifies us as 'fit' for the world we yearn.

More specifically, the journey does not end there or at the close of our lives on earth when we draw our last human breath. The yearning is always there, a longing to understand ourselves, a search for our roots, not that which is here from our birth but something earlier than that . . . in our creation, in the creation of man, in our Creator in eternity past. Has man always been so imperfect, so stained with blemishes, corruptible . . . bruised, helpless, and broken, never able to escape the bondage into which we are born? He is transient, here now and gone thereafter, forever. There have been times he waxed strong only to decline into oblivion, no ability to ward off the tendencies of frailty in his body and in his soul, and to hold off infirmity and decay. Living is but a mere *three score and ten years, and four score by virtue of strength:* long by clock time yet short when lived. Plunged in the vicissitudes, cares, entanglements, life robbed of its breath—the little he has done and the little that he can now do—justifies not the creative purpose for which his Creator has in mind. He is in a dreadfully mournful sorry state indeed.

In the age of discovery, as we grow older we become more cautious, more worldly-wise, more deliberate, more prudent; perhaps to protect us from the uncharted, the unknown. Everything seems to beg of a purpose of a goal, measurable in quantitative terms judged and passed according to the standards set by the system. The innocent abandonment, the childlike disregard of judgement suddenly cannot take root. One simply cannot ignore it. The measurements bug, gnawing away at one's soul until one gives in, in resignation. One simply cannot fight it. One becomes a convention not an un-convention; an acceptable exception if only on the side of convention. It is as 'all roads lead to Rome'; hop on the bandwagon to get there.

In the age of discovery, we grow older and we become more cautious, more worldly-wise, more deliberate, more prudent; perhaps to protect us from the uncharted, the unknown. Everything seems to beg of a purpose of a goal, measurable in quantitative terms judged and passed according to the standards set by the system. The innocent abandonment, the childlike disregard of judgement suddenly cannot take root. One simply cannot ignore it.

This book and the others to follow, the author prays, will enable us to see how far we have gone and perhaps reveal how far we should go. The *age of innocence* is past and over, gone and beyond re-living, the *age of discovery* draws nigh and shall duly pass on as well. Events past and over are lost when we leave them to oblivion as though they never existed. Times to come shall suffer the same fate. Unless we apply a conscious diligence to reflect on them, to make sense of them, and spur us to conscious determinate action, we truly live impoverished lives devoid of meaning and purpose. This book, the author hopes, will move us from enjoying the individual *experiences* in the times of our lives, and through diligent reflection to wholly understanding a *concept* of life: from the 'little bundle' of big things to the 'big bundle' of little things. *Prettily clear little ink drops become a big amorphous smudge on the blotting paper pressed over them.* The little ink drops in our lives pass on, drawn into, and become part of that big blob; reflect on the drops lest we lose sight of them as they infuse in the blob without trace of their beginnings. At the end of our lives, we may not have to consider passing off into the unknown, into oblivion. Reflection will let us see that we have beginnings for the same earthly ends with which we will come to face one day. *I call to remembrance my song in the night: I commune with mine own heart: and my spirit made diligent search.*—Psalms 77:6. In those beginnings, there must be A BEGINNING . . . *In the beginning, God created the heaven and the earth.*—Gen 1:1.

Endnotes

The beginning that God gave to man, man could not keep: man in his disobedience acted against God's character and against God's nature: man sinned. Disobedience is a rebellion against God's righteousness. God in His righteousness must necessarily mete out justice; He judges sin, and punishes absolutely: His righteousness abhors sin. Man henceforth lived under the bondage of sin, apart from God, under the curse of spiritual death caught in a vicious cycle of corruption rooted in his nature, unable to free himself from that bondage. Under the unrelenting hold of sin, he lives in darkness and cannot perceive the light that only God bestows. He has no hope of redeeming himself from God's judgment. God knows it. God in His infinite mercy covers man's sin and guilt—man's lifelessness, helplessness, absolute hopelessness, man's spiritual death—by giving man His only begotten Son as the only acceptable means of redemption from the wrath of His judgment on man's sin, so as to reconcile man to Him. *In the beginning was the Word, and the Word was with God, and the Word was God. The same was in the beginning with God. All things were made by him; and without him was not anything made that was made. In him was life; and the life was the light of men. And the light shineth in darkness; and the darkness comprehended it not . . . And the Word was made flesh, and dwelt among us, (and we beheld his glory, the glory as of the only begotten of the Father,) full of grace and truth.*—John 1:1-5, 14.

There was the beginning when God created the heaven and the earth the first man made from dust, into which God breathes His Spirit. In disobedience, *natural* man acquired the knowledge of good and evil. Henceforth, natural man lives and dies *in* sin. He separates from God and walks in darkness. There was the beginning of the *spiritual* man when God's only begotten Son came, live, and die as man so that *whosoever believes in Him should not perish but have everlasting life.* The Son of God yields His will for the Father's will and in obedience went to the cross. Man will no longer walk to the flesh; man can now walk in the Spirit of God. Man can now walk in the light and comprehend the light. He is regenerated as in a new birth, the old sinful man now overcame; a new man is raised in the nature of the Son of God, that we may be made the righteousness of God in Christ Jesus. *Who gave himself for us, that he might redeem us from all iniquity, and purify unto himself a peculiar people, zealous of good works.*—Titus 2:14. *Knowing that you were ransomed from the futile ways inherited from your forefathers, not with perishable things such as silver or gold, but with the precious blood of Christ, like that of a lamb without blemish or spot. He was foreknown before the foundation of the world but was made manifest in the last times for the sake of you who through him are believers in God, who raised him from the dead and gave him glory, so that your faith and hope are in God.*—1 Peter 1:18-21. *The thief comes only to steal and kill and destroy. I came that they may have life and have it abundantly. I am the good shepherd. The good shepherd lays down his life for the sheep.*—John 10:10-11.

Buy the truth, and sell it not; also wisdom, and instruction, and understanding.—Proverbs 23:23 . . . *whatsoever things are true, whatsoever things are honest, whatsoever things are just, whatsoever things are pure, whatsoever things are lovely, whatsoever things are of good report; if there be any virtue, and if there be any praise, think on these things.*—Philippians 4:8.

A rich green short hillock such as Mount Faber may lowly consider the anthill at its foot. When in the midst of a Kota Kinabalu (KK), the comparison between Mount Faber and the anthill fades and dissipates. The Pharisee holds the law in his pharisaical standard; the publican turned his head down in dejection and shame. Before a holy God, they are both sinners. The world's standards made no difference with God. However, what matters to God is the heart: that which is as the Pharisee's, thanking God by lifting himself in self-conceit with the proclamation that "I am not as other man"; or as the publican's dejected and sorrowful heart that humbly says, "God, be merciful to me a sinner." *Two men went up into the temple to pray, one a Pharisee and the other a tax collector. The Pharisee, standing by himself, prayed thus: 'God, I thank you that I am not like other men, extortioners, unjust, adulterers, or even like this tax collector. I fast twice a week; I give tithes of all that I get.' But the tax collector, standing far off, would not even lift up his eyes to heaven, but beat his breast, saying, 'God, be merciful to me, a sinner!'*—Luke 18:10-13.

Reflection humbles us. Reflection reveals our complete unworthiness. Reflection manifests the *nature* of our transgression, for we have walked in darkness, and shows how depraved we have been. Reflection informs categorically that we have no means of our own or of this world to overcome the very perverted nature that has dogged us relentlessly since our very first thought and act of disobedience. As *natural* man we are physically doomed, we are eternally lost . . . . Reflection desires out of this endless vicious sin cycle . . . Reflection searches and hungers for truth . . . for liberty . . .

HOW THIS BOOK IS ORGANISED

───◆⟡◆───

*A*ge of Discovery is organised quite differently from that in *Age of Innocence*. The events and experiences at home and at the new school RI (short for Raffles Institution) have become quite unlike those in the age of innocence. What used to be individual *events* with similar-level type of experiences for the six years at Jervois East, they have now become more like *scenes* quite new, more shocking than surprising, the environment more daunting, alarming, formidable, and larger than life. That once seen through the reporting eyes of *innocence* is now through the questioning eyes of *discovery*. The culture was a lot more independent than we were accustomed to at Jervois East. Where we once took instructions and acted in absolute obedience and adherence, we now took charge and were accountable to ourselves, our guides (teachers), our team, our organisation, the pride of our school, *the* premier learning institution. We are no longer islands to ourselves, we are variously connected and related to all we encounter and interact. Our homes and families become relatively dislocated as we seek to make sense of what we are experiencing in the world of schooling.

A prevailing emotion, sensibility that lasts longer, lingers, and is experienced over several encounters. It is not short and gotten over quickly. It stays, and hovers over one's spirit; it tarries. It is unlike a bird flying over our heads, but as one seeking to brood and nest in our hair. There is no driving it away immediately; it goes away when its stay is accomplished.

The organisation of this book centres on the change in the age of discovery so that it becomes the theme. The individual years, more a convenience associated with the education system, juxtapose the central theme of this book.

The Age of Discovery explores the period as one of a new experience with the rich history of RI as the true foundation of education in the vision of its founders, how that history continued to the present in RI being the flag bearer, the premier school of the nation. An institution of such illustrious character must have had an influence on all those who passed through its portals, bathed in its history, immersed in its very culture, soaked in its traditions, received instruction at its very excellent system, and showered by its rich legacy. In a sense, it reveals the diversity that became the outgrowth of that unity of vision and history. That diversity represents what Singapore was and is today: a melting pot of people who came from its neighbouring nations and those other more distant Asian nations. They made up the main racial composition of Chinese the majority, followed by Malays, and Indians next. For the first time in his life the author experienced history or a sense of history, the history of an institution in the history of a nation, how they intertwined, how they seemed destined for each other with a purpose, having a definite future. History is no longer about events of the past, not about dates: history is about now and what lies ahead. Will it be? Only time tells.

He considers expectations and their influence during the age of discovery in the context of his schooling, of his home, of the society he functions in, and the bigger world that adds a new dimension to his understanding, a world he knows of from the news, and readings he has access to, a limited world view one may think. He only lacks the experience.

The organisation of this book centres on the change in the age of discovery so that it becomes the theme. The individual years, more a convenience associated with the education system, juxtapose the central theme of this book.

He discovers much about the goings on in society: the economics of living as an individual, a family, as a nation, and in the context of the world: their inter-relationships, their interdependencies. Where once he knows little of the world and even with the advent of television, the broad news he receives is just that, having little impact on him at his age of innocence. However, now he gets more of it and the details of it: from big happenings down to world views down to trends, norms, at the societal level. It is not only about an awesome deluge of information and complexity, it is about making sense of them in the context of who he is, what he is to be and of how he can deal with it. The world and its happenings had agitated his young mind and begun to work on his points of view.

He also realises that what information he receives may take the slant of the reporting—newspapers, magazines, or television—their highlights, emphasis, sense of urgency, or national promotion. Vigilance, a necessary virtue to discern and divide asunder the influences upon life of which some lands on the soul, some skims off the surface, some pins only skin deep to shrug off easily, and some to scar for life. All the happenings about him were beginning to compete for his time and energy amidst the school workload. He cannot just pore over his school books, and tear away from these other things that engaged him; there was just too much happening about and around him in the world. He did not consider them a demand for they were 'real', alive, and deserved consideration by their very existences though they were inconsequent to his studies. He cannot change the world, thinking about the issues were a way of being involved in them in spirit, raising the emotions that flocked around them—anger, frustration, hopelessness, unfairness—that begun to foster a *discovery* of human nature, of the purpose of human life in the happenings. Most importantly, he seems to lose the *innocent* curiosity that drives his forward outlook. The legs are as leaden with suspecting questions, stuck in the miry clay that holds down any desire to flee, some hidden grievances about why things were the way they were, begun to surface.

Each chapter is organised in the chronology of the four years of secondary education in RI. In each chapter, the sections or subtitles expose salient mentions in that year of the author's time at RI, and ends with questions and musings further elucidated or expanded in the **Endnotes** of the author's musings and/or **References** of content/materials used may appear at the end of each chapter where necessary or appropriate.

PROLOGUE

———⟡———

*Though the fig tree should not blossom, nor fruit be on the vines,
the produce of the olive fail and the fields yield no food,
the flock be cut off from the fold and there be no herd in the stalls,
yet I will rejoice in the LORD; I will take
joy in the God of my salvation.*
—Habakkuk 3:17-18

From a simple, neat, trouble-free age of innocence, the author moves to something troubling: it is as a trial, an unavoidable trial necessary for one's growth and development from a child to a teenager to a youth, a gauntlet for the very young warrior. One might think of it as riding a roller coaster that begins from the high of innocence rolling steeply down into *shock and denial* in response to a new complexity. Unable to make sense of it he rolls on down to meet *depression and anger* in response to seeming chaos and disorder. From whence, he goes down further to the bottom *hanging on* in perseverance. Seeing possibilities in dealing with challenges, he rebounds towards *hope and acceptance* of the new system by adjusting to, participating in, and learning it. With hope, he undertakes *re-building* from new complexity to simplicity through a sensible articulation of vision and strategies to reach the end. The slide between the highs and lows of the roller coaster is wider, more variable, more marked, much longer . . . and . . . slower. There is more to mull over, more time to consider, digest, and assimilate. Being oneself was no longer easy as the voices of things, of people, of circumstances, of principles crowd about for attention and inclusion in one's deliberation and decision. We become an adaptation of all around us—friends, family, school, activities, the books, the system, the news, the expectations, our own limitations, our beliefs—we become a product constantly seeking out our true self, failing which we choose the path of least resistance. We become more like the world we live in. being different was odd, out-of-place, out-of-whack. Living becomes play acting on the world's stage. We lose ourselves. We lose our innocence. We lose our individuality. We think like the world. We have strings attached to our bodies and souls, tugging and loosening, influencing our thoughts and emotions. Drawn into the world, we live like the world. We live for the world, and for the things of the world.

Why was one at RI? Was it on one's own merits or in the Creator's design? In the larger scheme of things, it is Providence. At the level of humanity, the laws of nature although allowed to proceed are subject to the governance of God's providence. Providence is the foreseeing care and guidance of God over the creatures of the earth when He omnisciently directs the universe and all affairs of humankind with wise benevolence: a property, a manifestation of His divine care and direction. There is a purpose unknown to us. There is His will we cannot comprehend. We see the obvious, the immediate cause-and-effect. We cannot see the trees from the woods. He sees past the cause with eternal care to the effect in His will. As an event itself it tells us little, however, as an event within episodes over time in relation to other events and episodes, one might catch a glimpse of the shape of things that have been, and a sense of purpose in their outcomes. Life is like a play seed on a game board of *weiqi* (an ancient Chinese board game of black and white seeds, and popularised in Japan as *Go*) that faces several hundreds of probable outcomes from just one move. These outcomes generated by its position of seeds relative to those of the opponent's in possible layers of foreseeable steps, are inter-related and interdependent. The opponent's next move, were it not considered earlier, could generate further possibilities. The *weiqi* configuration is as the highly intelligent neuron networks in our human brain, only significantly less complex. The marvellous thing is that the moves are interrelated and interdependent: one move causes others to affect another as though in a predisposed configuration not easily read by an untrained eye or mind. The moves a player make generate measurable outcomes to decide the winner. It is as if all the little moves that man makes to affect change: destruction or flourish, pain or joy, loss or gain, hate or love, death or life, there is the foreknowing hand of God to caringly arrange outcomes in accord with His good and merciful will. Who can conceive all that but the Creator and Designer? *He made all things, and without him was not anything made, that was made.*

Being oneself was no longer easy as the voices of things, of people, of circumstances, of principles crowd about for attention and inclusion in one's deliberation and decision. We become an adaptation of all around us—

Yet in all this time at RI, things were, as the fig tree should not blossom, where the labour of the olive shall fail . . . where there was no herd in the stall. At the end, the author was able to rejoice just being in RI, of effort, in God's Will and thence His Providence. A review of this period of life at RI aimed to look at the lack of 'blossom', the lack of harvest, emptiness in the 'stall' as purposeful in its engagement of the author's development in thought and of the heart. It was as a period of kindly gestation to assimilate that which whirled about him in time, in the societal stage he was placed, and how he responded—cautiously, then more surely—and the *discovery* of where his affections lay at that time. The author was as a *natural* man sowing and reaping according to the laws of nature, of cause and effect; yet he was under the oversight of an Almighty God who in His Providence foreknowingly directs the course of events, through His allowing and or constraining/restraining the laws of nature to operate.

Therefore, is my spirit overwhelmed within me; my heart within me is desolate. I remember the days of old; I meditate on all thy works; I muse on the work of thy hands.—Psalm 143:4-5 . . . *a land of darkness, as darkness itself; and of the shadow of death, without any order, and where the light is as darkness.*—Job 10:22

1

A New Experience: History and Diversity

That which was from the beginning, which we have heard,
Which we have seen with our eyes,
Which we have looked upon,
And our hands have handled, of the Word of life.
—1 John 1:1

When Sir Stamford Raffles decided to build a premier educational institution, the vision was to make Singapore a centre of learning and that to a considerable extent the Institution would contribute to the better age to come, to serve the country well. He wanted to 'infuse into' RI a 'portion of that spirit and soul' he had for expanding the reach of the British East India Company.

This vision was for the Institution to be the Hope of a Better Age, encoded in the school's Latin motto, *Auspicium Melioris Aevi*.

Being the oldest school in Singapore from which many national leaders and prominent figures were 'raised and bred' educationally, an awesome unseen spirit or force had breathed a deep sense of pride in RI living its vision, in the supposed quality of its education system, its undying quest for excellence as manifested in its proud continuous history of achievements. The Rafflesian Spirit is, according to its website www.ri.edu.sg "a feeling that stems from the mind as well as the heart. It is a feeling of belonging to a great and magnificent institution with a proud heritage. It is a sense of togetherness that binds and inspires Rafflesians to give their best and reach for excellence."

The Institution's school song *Auspicium Melioris Aevi* though penned in this century a few decades ago tells what RI stood for, perhaps as a fitting afterthought of its motto.

> " . . . a feeling that stems from the mind as well as the heart. It is a feeling of belonging to a great and magnificent institution with a proud heritage. It is a sense of togetherness that binds and inspires Rafflesians to give their best and reach for excellence. "

Unity is the absence of diversity, the state of being one, oneness, concord, harmony, agreement. Diversity is being diverse, different, unlike, various, dissimilar, change. Can they ever align in a divisive world? The unity of vision that Raffles had, found a practical commonality with the bearers of it in generations thereafter, that allowed it to thrive in the diversity of the elements and the ensuing change. There was a seeming viable principle of co-existence with its changing environment through adjustments in the relationship of interdependence. The vision of a man limited in so many ways—in time and age; in space (sub-regional versus today's global), and in far better defined stages of development—can only meet its demise for an interfacing vision of its own time and space to run the race. That vision lives generally as an institution, a tradition of pride in its past; moved and acted out specifically on the world's stage of times and age. That vision did not make all that had happened. It shared its past glory with all those who were associated with it, became a part of it, who passed through its portals, who chanted its name, who hung on to it with pride regardless of the good and/or notoriety each carried by their lives in the changing world where they manifest themselves. All that man designed can only be temporal. There can be no unity in the Raffles vision to that future which carves for itself another vision, all that remains is a memory institutionalised in tradition.

How has RI been a distinctive influence on the author's life?

- A powerful history and status as the premier educational institution of the nation imbued in everyone who passed under its shadow a deep pride of having made it, of being a piece of the enduring legacy that made one 'special', as one raised and trained among the prime not by virtue of any high bequeathed social status or nobility. It was on the basis of meritorious selection and entry, fed through the furnace of extreme rigour, tempered, and shaped to excellent standards fit for use in the best of purposes. History offers a point of definite reference, its successful past as an anchor in turbulent times to continue surging forward into untested waters. *For enquire, I pray thee, of the former age, and prepare thyself to the search of their fathers: For we are but of yesterday, and know nothing, because our days upon earth are a shadow: Shall not they teach thee, and tell thee, and utter words out of their heart?*—Job 8:8-10

- The Rafflesian spirit that ensued from its history, position, and continuing achievements as though success builds on success, success breeds its own, there was no pause to think of, or consider slipping from that perch, as symbolised in the eagle eye and gryphon strength. There was a deep self-fulfilling prophecy of its continuing attainments . . . . *the protection of wisdom is like the protection of money, and the advantage of knowledge is that wisdom preserves the life of him who has it.*—Ecclesiastes 7:12

- A sense of calling to that destiny, to that future hope for a better age, sets on him the badge of servant-hood a time-honoured sense of responsibility. *He chose our heritage for us, the pride of . . . whom he loves.*—Psalm 47:4.

- A need to uphold its spirit of excellence as one called to that task, no slackening entertained, no dodging or desertion of accountability harboured. *My son, eat honey, for it is good, and the drippings of the honeycomb are sweet to your taste. Know that wisdom is such to your soul; if you find it, there will be a future, and your hope will not be cut off.*—Proverbs 24:13-14.

- A self-expectation to count among the best requires of him a definite commitment to that role. *For surely there is an end; and thine expectation shall not be cut off.*—Proverbs 23:18.

With who are we in unity? Was it with Raffles? Students came from all over the country, and they went away to local and/or foreign universities year in year out. Some returned home to enter the public service, many to the private business organisations. Infused with that peculiar Rafflesian character that went to its calling wherever we ultimately work our way, we were in a sense, in unity to the Rafflesian call. Raffles Institution was not an educational institution that propagated an English aristocratic air. We did not profess to dress, talk, and behave like the English gentleman. We were simply ordinary folks, all endowed differently in material trappings or poverty, in intelligence or abilities of sorts, driven to be the best, and hence going to the best place of education to be among the best, clearly a simple model of practicality—in living, in doing what was naturally necessary.

Was unity with God? And was it with a particular God? That last line in *Auspicium Melioris Aevi* 'with God to guide the way' had often baffled me. RI was not a Christian school. For a Buddhist

I have no God and that attribution to an English God was offensive. Was 'God' here a generic term to mean a higher power, a higher unknown power that believers and non-believers embrace? Was God just a pass-on, a legacy from our English founders? With God's place on the last line of the song, He appears as the sovereign Providence who in His infinite wisdom and foreseeing care, guides our vision, our steps forward. For an unchanging vision, it has to exude from an immutable entity.

With what were we in unity? Was it with a vision? Was it with a reality? Raffles had his vision/dream drawn from his broad mandate from the East India Company, translated that into an immediate and intermediate mission that could bring that vision into reality. It was no longer just an idea; it now tempered with the things he saw on the ground, their true conditions, their challenges, their possibilities, and the extent of reach to them. How can a small island carry the region's trade as Atlas lifting the world on his shoulders?

What was our diversity? Can the Chinese, the Indian, the Malay, and others speak, write, behave, and think as Englishmen? Can we communicate with them as one? Can this diversity integrate? History had for thousands of years seen segregation of cultures, and with the conquests of nations, attempts at integration became possible through constituted common laws for governance to enable wieldy rule. Yet history had often in the past shown assimilation difficult, the long deep roots of culture, race, and language have fire-walled it.

Great empires and dynasties have come and gone, all became history: Babylonian, Assyrian, Mede-Persian, Grecian, Roman, Mongolian (and all the Chinese dynasties), Byzantine, Ottoman . . . what have they achieved for man in his purpose as man? The human race seemed to live in an endless perpetuation of times past of history, won and failed, only to start another and another . . . a continuing succession of repeated lessons that man had manifestly failed to learn and master.

Our birth and destiny in the small island state of Singapore is the English system. We have our roots in China, India, Malaya, or anywhere else, where our forefathers came from but as history fades, we only know this as our place of birth, and where we grew up, built a life upon, and ultimately rest. Can we be as good as the English? Will we be like them? We can copy them. Are they the ultimate? Perhaps, it appears to be at that point in history. Can we better them? Why should we? We do our best with the English language and the average Singaporean cannot raise his proficiency in it; we have lost much of our Chinese language while pursuing English. We are neither here nor there, in 'no man's land'. We can say the same of our culture and traditions. Are we subconsciously attempting to create a Singapore identity that is not naturally inherent but one variously adopted? Is that an identity? On the other hand, can unchanging traditions hold places in an open dynamically changing world where myriads of other traditions commingle to make sense for the times?

Endnotes

Change in itself speaks of impermanence. It seeks to adjust, to moderate, and to adapt according to altering states and conditions. In the state we are in, our lives can only be impermanent. Is all purpose then to that end? The history of mankind begun in perfection by God's decree went through the gamut of corruption by man's wilfulness, only raised to perfection at the end by Christ's restoration.

Truly, at the end of it all, it is not time and space, nor the state of technology in the ages, that hold the reins and sway of history. It is all about man, the state, and condition of man. Very specifically, it is the moral state of man that determines the present state of things, and that of times to come. *The heart is deceitful above all things, and desperately wicked: who can know it? I the LORD search the heart, I try the reins, even to give every man according to his ways, and according to the fruit of his doings.*—Jeremiah 17:9-10.

For who among them has stood in the council of the LORD to see and to hear his word, or who has paid attention to his word and listened? Behold, the storm of the LORD! Wrath has gone forth, a whirling tempest; it will burst upon the head of the wicked.—Jeremiah 23:18-19.

"Am I a God at hand" declares the LORD, "and not a God far away? Can a man hide himself in secret places so that I cannot see him?" declares the LORD. "Do I not fill heaven and earth?" declares the LORD.—Jeremiah 23:23-24.

References
E. Wijeysingha, *One Man's Vision: Raffles Institution in Focus*, Raffles Institution 1992.

E. Wijeysingha, *The Eagle Breeds a Gryphon: The Story of Raffles Institution, 1823-1985*, Pioneer Book Centre 1962.

Under the Banyan Tree: Collected Memories of Some Inspiring Rafflesians (1961-1964), Raffles Institution 2007.

1.1 Location, vicinity, and travelling

RI was located in the central business district (CBD) amidst major historical, government, and commercial landmarks. It was a district that represented strategic positioning of the well-placed deep water harbour front, a reminder of Singapore's beginnings as a preferred port of call for ships from the West to the East, and vice versa. The CBD was where the seat of government manifested itself in the City Hall, Parliament House, Supreme Court, and the General Post Office. Further along the stretch was the banking and financial district. I have walked into many of these buildings, climbed up their many floors to sell funfair tickets to raise funds for the new RI Building Fund.

RI sat on a closely square piece of land flanked by four major and busy roads. Bras Basah Road separated RI from the side of Raffles Hotel. Stamford Road separated RI from the Anglican St. Andrew's Cathedral, with the Stamford canal between it and the road. Beach Road ran between RI and the less than peaceful lonesome War Memorial amidst the noisy heavy motor traffic, while North Bridge Road kept the rather cloistered CHIJ (Convent of the Holy Infant Jesus) at bay, a curious place that shut itself in from the busy world outside. CHIJ was a school for girls, not a convent as its name suggested. Capitol Theatre was at the corner of North Bridge Road and Stamford Road, facing diagonally across the RI school field, its design not quite Victorian, simply hybrid. The Victoria Memorial Hall, Parliament House, The Supreme Court, and City Hall ran along Saint Andrew's Road. Past that was Anderson Bridge spanning the narrow feed of the Singapore River, with Fullerton Road leading to the banking and commercial district.

Favourite haunts that many Rafflesians went to were the Capitol Theatre, the War Memorial, and the Indian bookstores along Bras Basah Road where we practised our skills at negotiating book prices, both new and second hand. One of our hot competitors, SJI (St. Joseph's Institution) sited along Bras Basah Road with Catholic High School at the adjacent Queen's Street. There were also several primary schools in the vicinity. Other major landmarks included the National Museum and the National Library. At Beach Road corner was the NAAFI (Navy, Army, and Air Force Institute) the British forces clubhouse. Still further up Bras Basah Road towards Orchard Road, along Dhoby Ghaut where Cathay Cinema was sited, and at the corner stood MacDonald House where terrorist bombs went off during the political merger (with Malaysia), ideological confrontation (with Indonesia), and political separation days of Singapore (from Malaysia). Opposite MacDonald House was the Amber Mansion. The landscape has changed today and several buildings are gone such as the National Library, and Amber Mansion, and RI of course where Raffles City now stands tall. The Indian bookstores have and disappeared and moved to Bras Basah Complex which faces North Bridge Road. Others had facelifts and their names changed: CHIJ is now CHIJMES (to sound like 'chimes'), SJI is today the Art Museum.

Mie arranged a pirate taxi (yes, a pirate taxi, not a spelling error; we could not afford a 'private' one) only for one month. Opposite from our house, our neighbour a very decent family man drives a pirate taxi and eventually switched to a metered taxi with the change of times. Mie arranged for him to send me to and from RI. He was very willing as he had three other new RI students in our vicinity. That lowered the cost for us. For me it was for the short first month until I was familiar with the route and better oriented. At the end of the first month, I was on my own and took buses to and from school.

Buses in those days had no air-conditioning, just open windows, glass windows that one could slide up or down along vertical spaces that serve to dovetail the glass on both its edges. Some of these windows from either wrong use or lack of maintenance was stuck in the worst places at the top, shutting out incoming air. If one had asthma or a low heart function, one would have dropped dead or died of asphyxiation. When not crowded they were well circulated, tolerable, and comfortable. However, during peak hours particularly on the trip from RI to home they always packed to overfull, violating the capacity requirements, and moving much too slowly. The body heat, the sticky sweaty skins, the odour of sweat shirts, the close hot breaths of fellow travellers, the crush, and the jostling in the tropical humid weather makes bus travel thoroughly an energy drain. It was generally a waste of time when the crowd simply was disagreeable with attempts to read even a few lines of a book. The Hock Lee Bus Company, the STC (Singapore Traction Company), and the Tay Koh Yat Bus Company operated these buses. The STC fleet of buses were newer and sturdier than that of the other two older bus companies, the design also more spacious. Hock Lee buses were really as old rickety giant boxes; some even had open back so passengers could hop on and hop off. These were rather dangerous for passengers, with other vehicular traffic tailing it. Each bus had a bus driver and a bus conductor. The conductor issued the ticket and collected the fares as passengers filed up the bus. When the bus was packed to over the approved capacity, the conductor could be at the front half of the bus collecting fares and punching tickets because some passengers climbed in by the open backdoor to secure a place on the bus. That meant passengers on a short trip who came in by the front could get off by the front and therefore got a free ride. This was a voluntary system where passengers called out the fares they were paying, the unscrupulous ones would call for a lower fare. There was just no way of checking. The bus companies used occasional inspectors in white uniforms to check on passengers; for them the hours of low passenger loads were best. It was funny how deterrent officers must have white tops. We did not have the concept of compliance officers then. Passengers were more unlikely to transgress in a normal ride but the understatement of fares was rife in packed buses where things were out of control. It was a time of chaos in the public transportation system, and I may say also of many other things, a young nation going through birth pangs and emerging into many uncharted areas of government and public administration. Private businesses also realised in good time that they needed to collaborate with the government's modernisation and productivity efforts.

Safety on the buses was an issue. Pickpockets were common on buses as they were in the night bazaars (pasar malam). On many occasions on the way home, I had to take a short bus trip to the Chulia Street terminal and from there changed to another for the long trip home. The short trip was overwhelmingly packed and I had to pull myself up on a sloping handrail of the bus' door with one leg on the stair for a foothold. My other leg hung loose on the outside of the bus and my schoolbag slung across my shoulder. When the bus cornered, I faced my biggest challenge when the turning torque required me to heave myself up and at the same time touch-step on the moving road surface as an aid to keep up. A poor synchrony with the road, the turning force, speed of the bus, and the strength of the one hand hanging on the rail could mean a fatal slip. A few scares of this nature convinced me to take the next bus whenever the current one was exceedingly packed. It meant reaching home when the skies have darkened, keeping Pa and Mie worried. It was an early lesson in physical risk management.

In the late morning in my first year at RI, when I no longer had the pirate taxi service, I walked from home to Redhill where the STC roadside bus terminal was, to take a straight bus to Bras Basah Road. Very often I was the first and only passenger to start the trip, more came on board along the way. That late morning walk had always been very lightening, after a shower and early lunch at home. I would dress smartly in my all-white school uniform of short-sleeved shirt with the proud green and black metallic school badge safety-pinned on the left and only pocket, and shorts; my hair neatly combed back and held down by Brylcreem hair cream. Brylcreem was white and soft, not particularly oily. Pa applied the green translucent sticky Yardley on my hair only on special occasions when the few 'stubborn' strands refused to stay down. I would pass the few pigs rolling in mud in the open grass-less piece of land before the bus terminal, and although an interesting sight to watch, I kept at a clear distance from them as they swished their muddy tails. When the ground was soft, I would walk in a more roundabout manner along stepping-concrete slabs to ensure my white school shoes would not suffer. These pigs were relatively large animals and I have often wondered if they could outrun me. The live moving pigs are a very rare sight these days except for those that lay motionless on the butchery's cutting boards, all slit open, clinically parted and attractively presented.

Endnotes

Location and vicinity speak of space defined by distance; travel speaks of distance measured by time. Space and time are as an inseparable twin all through earthly life. When our soul breathes its last breath, the body corrupts, returns to dust; the soul, the spirit flees to eternity . . . spelling the end of space and time? It is certainly the case when you are God's, when you acknowledge him; when you believe in Christ as the Lord of your life, in that He redeemed/ purchased you from the bondage of sin He died on the cross to bear God's wrath over your sins, so that you are adopted as sons into His Kingdom. God purchased you for Himself. *Then shall the dust return to the earth as it was: and the spirit shall return unto God who gave it.*—Ecclesiastes 12:7.

1.2 Enrolment mix

At RI, we had some Indian students both dark and fair-skinned, lots of Chinese, some Malays, and even fewer Eurasians that one can number on the fingers of one hand. A sweeping view of the student population and mix might offer a reasonably representative perspective of the social-political construct with reference to races in Singapore. The pattern has not changed, and the proportions have altered somewhat for reasons that may have to do with economic and social engineering within the natural constraints of geography, history, and the times.

This construct apparently followed us throughout much of our lives, have worked well and little disruption anticipated. Again, that is just in our particular lifetime. Will this continue? Whether we know it or not, there has always been a subconscious consideration in the background that lent itself to little concern in a well-managed political-social-economic environment. The construct stresses of the past have been too far behind for this generation now to remember until perhaps when . . . *the night is far spent, the day is at hand.* The challenges are closely similar in most multi-racial, multi-ethnic communities and nations in their development, whether engineered or organic. However, we still have many lessons from which to learn of the possible-impossible, and the controllable-uncontrollable. Man cannot play God for man will not let man play God. God will not let man be God: He made man lower than Him. God made man for His own pleasure.

Secondary one classes, identified as A to H, eight classes each with forty pupils gives a total of three hundred and twenty pupils all in one afternoon session of secondary ones. With three secondary levels, one to three, that is a total of nine hundred and sixty pupils. In the morning session, which housed the secondary fours, pre-university ones and twos, the numbers are about equivalent. The classrooms for secondary one were located on the ground floor while the secondary twos took the second or upper floor of the main block; the annexe block accommodated the secondary threes.

1.3 Physical size and the buildings

RI was easily three to four times the size of Jervois East. The school field was a large visible dull green with barren patches of earth about the football goal posts and along the edge on one side of the field where regular leg traffic had choked the life of the struggling grass: one could make out the receding boundary on one side of the field. It appeared particularly daunting during the hot and dry spells when water from hoses provided brief reprieve for the yellowing, desperately choked grass straining for every bit of moist in a dry beaten barren hard ground.

The main block was a long continuous block with the central protruding sub-block wider and longer than the other two on both its side. This wide and long protrusion was the school hall extended outwards so it was large to accommodate the whole school attendance during assemblies. The rest of the main block housed the classrooms and the library. All floors were of bare wooden strips with the grooves in between them clearly visible with the dirt and dust of time. One wondered why there appeared a sense of thoughtlessness and carelessness in the design and construction of a historic landmark of a premier educational institution. Some years later, it probably was not painful to let the buildings come down and have RI move to a more modern facility. These old buildings could not qualify for historic preservation.

The admin block was rectangular in shape at right angles to the main block and three-storied topped with a sloping orange-coloured interlocking tiled roof that covered over like a hat. It contained the principal's office, teachers' common room, and the general office. Much of the topmost floor accommodated the school band: its practice or concert room, quartermaster's store, music scores library, musical instruments store, etc. Just like all these old buildings, there were no acoustics, just echoes everywhere. This topmost floor can be eerie in the very early morning hours like five o'clock when day had not quite broken, and winds run right through the open-meshed windows passing through the interconnecting labyrinth of small rooms and the larger concert room. I had opportunities to experience this chilling feel for many years when the band was involved in the National Day Parades requiring us to come early to prepare and dress up. This nook was a memorable one for me, it was where the bandmaster heard a mysteriously well-toned lone trumpeter that attracted and pleased his ears. He tracked it down in the smaller room and was surprised that it came from me the euphonist. From then on, I played in the first trumpet section. I finally played the instrument of my choice.

This topmost floor was also the place we the fortunate few gathered to watch major games of rugby, football, and softball on the field just right in front of the admin block. We had the premium 'circle' seats with the bird's eye view. Still there were times when we could not resist the thrills of close-up participation on the sidelines of the field. That topmost floor was where the school band had its headquarters, store, and practice rooms.

There were occasions when we practised together out in the open dusty area between the admin and science blocks, vacated with the demolition of an old block that had wide deep gaping cracks in its frontal walls. Having band practice there was a poor alternative, it was in the open air, temporarily under the shadow of the admin block when the sun was rising. When the sun rose high, we had to adjust our positions. After the building's demolition, the school administration did not tar or grass over the area, and left it a barren and dusty sight. Access to the band's nook was through an internal narrow winding staircase at the right side of the block, only the band had the key to open the little door at this access.

The annexe or science block was where the science laboratories were on the ground floor along with classrooms in the upper floor. It stood to the right of the open space vacated by the demolished block. Annexed to it was the Annexe canteen or tuck shop, a busy gathering and 'watering' point for all. All buildings were white-washed and carried the similar Victorian theme. Roofs were triangles, topped with unglazed orange-coloured interlocking tiles to allow rainwater to flow into gutters and down galvanized zinc pipes into the drains on the ground. The unglazed tiles had attracted unsightly patches of dirt and moss to cling to from years of neglect, begging a timely scrub down. The buildings looked very tall but were of two storeys because they had very high ceilings like double what we have at home. In the same design theme of the time they were constructed, all had wooden floor strips. Only the canteens were single storied.

These RI buildings, from afar, looked resplendent in their near pure white and Victorian majesty. However, on close scrutiny there was very little that was aesthetic in its design, nothing fine in its workmanship: no intricate contours, no elaborate capitals on grand columns, even the words 'RAFFLES INSTITUTION' and the second line 'FOUNDED 1823' were unceremonious, shallowly and shyly engraved on the plain triangular capital of the main building. The materials used were probably a mix of large blocks of cut stones wrapped in sand and limestone. Occasional sections of wall in years of wearing away had revealed the faint shape of those blocks. Limestone was obvious as some corners, ceilings, and walls showed visible signs of water seeping, penetrating, pushing through, and looking for every weak pore to initiate new accesses in the material. It was as though RI built in a hurry with an unwilling budget, was simply a dream built on bare-boned resources, the cost not counted, and probably a dream not fully backed by the powers that be. The buildings eventually gave way to economically feasible alternatives of greater significance to modernisation. I have learnt to appreciate the tug between the old and the new, between traditions and new conventions, between history and the present/future, between stagnation and proliferation. Al this is not merely in the 'life' of a building, an institution but also in men's lives. *"Why do you call me*

15

'Lord, Lord,' and not do what I tell you? Everyone who comes to me and hears my words and does them, I will show you what he is like: he is like a man building a house, who dug deep and laid the foundation on the rock. And when a flood arose, the stream broke against that house and could not shake it, because it had been well built. But the one who hears and does not do them is like a man who built a house on the ground without a foundation. When the stream broke against it, immediately it fell, and the ruin of that house was great."—Luke 6:46-50.

1.4 Extra-curricular activities

ECA for short, extra-curricular activities counted as part of the total education. The points attained became like a 'helping' grade when your other grades were not great for a major decision to move one up the education ladder. Grade 1 was not difficult to attain when one was a member of a uniformed group as it was a mainstay in many of the school's activities like Sports Day, Founder's Day, National Day, and the like. The military band contributed to 70% of my ECA grade. Other contributions came from memberships to clubs and societies, inter-class and inter-unit (inter uniformed group) competitions: in debating, athletics, and sport. Uniformed groups included the National Cadet Corps, Police Cadet Corps, Military Band, Scouts, and the Red Cross. Participation in a uniformed group or a sport category was the foundation of ECA.

Sports at school level covered Athletics, Rugby, Softball, Football, Hockey, Cricket, Table Tennis, Tennis, Badminton, and Sepak Takraw (cane ball). Football became Soccer; Hockey then played on grass with wooden sticks, today it is played on artificial water-based astro turf and is a very fast game, the ball is now like a giant golf ball with dimples, and the sticks contain a composite of wood, glass or carbon fibre, and therefore lighter, more sensitive, and stronger. Squash was unheard of until a few years later when

RI moved to the Grange Road site. For tennis, we only had a clay court then, so when you see someone's white school shoes looking orangey red, you were almost certain he had been playing tennis.

Clubs and Societies varied, formed under the disciplines and included English and Chinese Language/Debating/Cultural Societies known as LDCS in short, Interact Club, History Society, Science Club, Geography Society, Mathematics Club, Photography, etc. The variety catered to the varied and diverse interests of its students.

Endnotes

ECA comprising the literary-cultural societies/clubs, the uniformed groups, with a predominant sport component, had become a part of the school education system. One can trace it to ancient times where they existed: the Chinese (who thought of it as physical training), Egyptians, and generally we think of the ancient Greeks where competitions held in Olympia in Peloponnesus became our Olympic Games. For the Greeks, it was about a beautiful balanced physique, skills, flexibility, and athleticism. Sport had the element of competition among individuals or groups of individuals competing on a fair and equitable basis absent from unethical hidden practices to affect the outcomes of the competition. Such unethical practices today include performance enhancing drugs, match fixing, and the use of unapproved equipment/technology. The more open fair play issues impacting sport in our times may include racism, violence, and politics. Over time sport had evolved into an activity that strives for greater performance (hence professionalism, more investments in technology to improve the body and the appliances/tools), and for recognition (both individual and group). More economic resources flow into sport, more people are entertained as spectators, and promoters profit from the higher revenues generated at the spectator gates. Prizes to sport athletes count in stratospheric pecuniary compensations. More people are spending more time in sport as participants, and as spectators (both 'live' and those who watched from recorded media). This inordinate expense of one's life lends attention to the body and to competition. What effect does this lay on man, on society, on the future? *I returned, and saw under the sun, that the race is not to the swift, nor the battle to the strong, neither yet bread to the wise, nor yet riches to men of understanding, nor yet favour to men of skill; but time and chance happeneth to them all.*—Ecclesiastes 9:11.

There might have been the view that the well-rounded man was a scholar, and athletic; the Chinese at some time in its history considered the scholarly (academia) man with pugilistic skills (sport). The great universities in the world promoted sport as an essential component in the education curriculum. For thousands of years this has similarly been embedded in our education system and therefore at RI, such that we take much pride in excelling in sport as rugby, hockey, cricket, and football, mostly of English origin brought in by our colonial government in the late 1800s to the early 1900s. one particular Christian school in Singapore had on its walls in huge lettering that in paraphrase urges its students to be . . . *a scholar, an officer, and a gentleman* . . . Surprising? The world cultivates a scholarly mind, a well-proportioned physique and healthy body, and an outwardly acceptable perception of manliness. Our Creator infuses His Spirit and cleans out our depraved spirit, endue us with His Spirit that we may live in His image, and in His nature that manifests His absolute standard of holiness apt to exact justice on transgressions, yet ever ready to forgive in mercy and compassion.

1.5 Style of education

Style is a fashion, a manner, custom, design, approach, convention, and framework. Style has to follow its vision moderated by the circumstances. Such vision crafted in the English tradition can only mean an education system framed or designed after what the English considered a 'good' education. Our own political leaders emerged from the English system, went to Oxbridge, LSE, and the like. We had little history concerning education of our own kind. The early core came from the British system and an extension of it; we still have the Cambridge General Certificate Examinations (GCE). RI was not an aristocratic independent all-boys boarding school such as Eton, Harrow, or Winchester; it was and still is a 'meritocratic' all-boys public school. RI, however, like Eton was the 'chief nurse of our nation's statesmen'. What a parallel.

Underlying education seems to be a desire to turn out people who will become *useful* to themselves and to society, well-rounded balanced individuals, as the educators would have it. The government embraces that and want education to produce the *rightly skilled* people for national and economic growth and development. The people want education only if they can make a *meaningful* living from having it. All look for the outcomes that will support a material life, a physical one, one about 'bread and butter', about subsistence, for human sustainability. What matters is the soul, the spirit in man . . . Ah! That has been the challenge since times immemorial. Man will not shut out the sirens; he will not close out his windows to the allures of the world. He lives for the *now*, he lives for *this* world. Man is not true to the truth. Man has lost the truth. Education has lost its way.

Endnotes

Education is learning in which knowledge, skills, and habits of a group of people transferred from one generation to the next through teaching, training, research, or simply through self-learning. Self-directed learning more specifically, which I now understand to mean auto-didacticism, seemed quite common in those days when one could enrol in a correspondence course to learn about electrical engineering and related technical subjects, and then take examinations regulated by City & Guilds (C&G) in the U.K. and invigilated in Singapore. Likewise, accountancy was similarly popular. There were local commercial schools in the evening that prepared part-time candidates for the London Chamber of Commerce (LCC), Pitman, ACCA (accountancy), and other accountancy examinations set in the U.K.

Generally, education occurs through any experience that has a formative effect on the way one thinks, feels, or acts. In Singapore, secondary education comprises the formal education that occurs during adolescence. Characterized by transition or progression from the compulsory, comprehensive primary education for minors aged between 7 and 12, to the selective tertiary, post-secondary, or higher education (e.g. university, vocational and technical school/polytechnic) for adults, its purpose was to give common knowledge, to prepare for higher education or to train directly in a profession.

Secondary, pre-university, polytechnic, and trade education for Singapore, at that time a young state in early nation building, was a critical area of government and economic policy making, due to the need to bring in large foreign investors such as big businesses that brought with them the technological advances in factories that required skilled workers. To meet this new specialised job demand, school curriculum focused on practical job skills that would better prepare students for white collar or skilled blue collar work. This was beneficial for both employers and employees, for improvement in human capital raised productivity, lowered costs for the employer; skilled employees received a higher wage than those with basic primary education. Engineering and technical education applied to industry was the urgent priority to ensure economic survival as the bread and butter, while the bacon waited a little.

"*Your child belongs to us already . . . . What are you? You will pass on. Your descendants, however, now stand in the next camp. In a short time they will know nothing else but this community."* (1933). *"This new Reich will give its youth to no one, but will itself take youth and give to youth its own education and its own upbringing."* (1937). Hitler in 1933 and 1937, was fully aware that the home could become the greatest threat to state ideology and ordered children into government schools. Was it so with our schools? Hitler and communist states were concerned with state ideology. Singapore was concerned with economic survival and building a social democracy of multiple races, religions, and languages, of varied ethnicities that required the will of the people to congregate around a national blueprint not of ideology but of practicality. The issues were bread and butter in nature and not of political or social ideas. RI was within the framework of a government school yet with a renowned vision and tried standards of excellence. There were loose-tight relationships between government and the governed, between ideology and utility, between law and freedom, between unity and diversity, between a need and a want, between science and the arts . . . a different tune for every different dance. The mandate was clear, there was little to choose.

I became an autodidact while at an early point in my life at RI. Auto didacticism is self-directed learning that is related to but different from informal learning. In a sense, auto didacticism is 'learning on your own' or 'by yourself', and an autodidact is a self-teacher. Auto didacticism is a contemplative, absorptive process requiring the learner to delve into, to dissect the subject, and build a framework of understanding the concepts. While informed in a conventional manner in the education system, I chose to inform myself in other, often unrelated areas. Resources were then limited and self-directed learning absorbed much of my time and energy, caused a digression, and promoted much reading outside the curriculum: they added little to my academic scores . . . . *Ever learning, and never able to come to the knowledge of the truth.*—2 Timothy 3:7. However, they did offer my young enquiring mind a wide repertoire of knowledge on varied subjects that allowed me to consider emerging issues seriously rather than lay them aside by reason of ignorance. In later years, looking back, self-learning combined with what I had in accessible resources enabled me to learn music, to learn to draw and paint, to play the trumpet and Chinese flute, to take up the study of accounting when medical school was beyond my reach, to learn to swim, to discover sprinting, and so on. When younger, Pa had always tinkered with broken things and re-used them. We do not always buy new things, we make old broken things work again. Pa was a wee bit of a self-learner from the practical side. There was a developed sense of adventurism and self-reliance. I believe the style of education at RI was akin to my early life, and played a big part in my embrace of auto didacticism, when there was no one else to learn from or be taught by, other than the school, which in a sense confined to examinable content. Perhaps it was like what a luminary once said about an educated man, as someone who need not know everything about anything but knew *where* to look for *what* he needed to know. Education at RI had 'educated' me.

Home-schooling is gaining popularity, driven by various forces, manifests self-directed learning characteristics. Its popularity driven in part by religious reasons, and also concerns in the less than desirable school environment, as well as dissatisfaction in the method of instruction. There has been a *change in the place* of learning: in home settings instead of at school. Students are, however, required to still participate in the national landmark examinations such as the Primary School Leaving Examinations (PSLE) at age 12, the General Certificate of Education Ordinary level (GCE 'O') at age 16, and the General Certificate of Education Advanced level (GCE 'A') examinations at age 18. Is homeschooling *isolation* from the world? I think not, in my knowledge and understanding of it. Is homeschooling a *separation* from the world? I should think so, to keep apart from undesirable influences within the school from fellow participants in the system; there is no conceivable way to prevent it without an integrated overhaul of the system vis-à-vis society at large. Can we live in the world and yet be separate from it? Can we keep ourselves apart from its influences? Is the separation a continuum? Can you deal with it? The things we touch daily, moment by moment—the computers, phone devices, the news on the air or in print, in the social media—are proliferated with information, accurate or slanted, tending to build up or to subvert, purposeful or frivolous. They impinge on our lives, on our decisions, on the principles, on the motivations in their use. Our backdrop of beliefs, our anchors, our foundations of conviction, will tend to be beacons of light emanating from the lighthouse. *"You are the salt of the earth, but if salt has lost its taste, how shall its saltiness be restored? It is no longer good for anything except to be thrown out and trampled under people's feet. "You are the light of the world. A city set on a hill cannot be hidden. Nor do people light a lamp and put it under a basket, but on a stand, and it gives light to all in the house. In the same way, let your light shine before others, so that they may see your good works and give glory to your Father who is in heaven.*—Matthew 5:13-16.

The Internet today, with its viral networks that pervade the world of information bringing on unimaginable availability and access not possible a decade or two ago. It peddles for free or at a price, all sorts of information and also products through and across it. The internet has now enabled lifelong education to be in terms of continuing development, and that makes for the feasibility of self-directed learning. One can learn the trumpet through a video lesson, read about health, research to supplement one's understanding of a medical condition, listening to a sermon or to music, watching a movie, reading a book, and practically anything else. It is almost all available 'on-demand' . . . the *place* is now *anywhere* and *anytime*. The gravest and consequential challenge lies in the validation of the content for accuracy, free from extraneous influences to slant and corrupt recipients of such content. The internet media's easy access subverts ethics, social mores, moral values, and religious doctrines through the elements that live in and by it. *And with many other words, did he testify and exhort, saying, save yourselves from this untoward generation.*—Acts 2:40

Reference

William L. Shirer, *The Rise And Fall Of The Third Reich: A History of Nazi Germany*, 1959.

1.6 Courses/subjects of study

In secondary one and two, the examinable courses studied were compulsory and included the following: English Language, English Literature, Chinese-as-second language, Mathematics, Science, Geography, History, and Art. When streaming into Arts or Science took place at secondary three, the Science stream required us to study the following examinable compulsory courses: English

Language, English Literature, Elementary Mathematics, Additional Mathematics, Chinese-as-second language, Physics, Chemistry, and Geography. The Science stream prepared us to enter the medical, pure science, economics, and engineering disciplines. The Arts stream generally thought of as leading to the study of arts, literature, linguistics, social science, law, government, philosophy, and political science.

2

Expectations

Be patient therefore . . .
Behold, the husbandman waiteth for the precious fruit of the earth,
And hath long patience for it, until he
receives the early and latter rain.
—James 5:7

What can one expect when posted out from an unknown school to one famously ensconced in the enclave of tradition and excellence, in the harbour of history proven and tested as the symbol of the ultimate in secondary education? What does one look forward to, anticipate, hope for, and trust in? What is the prospect of the future, what is the outlook? Expectations begin at the place arrived, the now, and looking towards that which lies before it. More than expectations, there was a thrilling anticipation of expectations becoming realities. Expectations . . . expectations . . . expectations, we cannot seem to live without them. They deliberately move us forward or hold us back, quickly or slowly, decisively or hesitatingly. They rule our every action, our every consideration. Expectations known define what must be, thus excite, vex and stress us; expectations unknown set us on the edge, taunt, and terrify us.

At the time of receiving posting orders to RI in December of the year earlier, there was a sense of belief, and of anticipation of better things ahead, things new, things to challenge me to discover more of what I had up to that very time in my life. There was much hope in great experiences and meaning. When on the trail of 'success' one can see little else but more success, as if that was one's ordered destiny, one's appropriated portion to proudly embrace. It did not matter who bestowed that destiny, be it God or the natural laws of cause and effect.

Upon entry on the first day, everything was to be different. Jervois East was a three hundred metre walk from home, so near and safe. RI was miles away, travelling one way by bus was an hour and more: as the pirate taxi driver lived opposite my home, I was the last to reach home by default. A month following entry to RI when I switched to buses, travelling became longer, and hazardous though unknown to Pa and Mie. I was particularly concerned about losing my bus fare before boarding the crowded buses. It was no paranoia for I actually lost my fare when riding home from the Chulia Street bus terminal. Reaching into my pocket for my fare after getting on the bus, I could not find it, and decided to alight after a few stops and walked home instead of facing the embarrassment of 'stealing' a free ride. For a while, I used my handkerchief to wrap the coin in one of its corner and tied a knot about it. That did the job.

The first week at RI was one of *apprehension* from coming face to face with unknown expectations. There was a certain stress and an intense suspense and excitement that set me on the edge. At the same time, there was such an overwhelming *assurance* of greatness in entering the portals of the ultimate school, along with the *assumption* of continued joyful breezy schooling life that I had at Jervois East.

Expectations have always been real. They have always been realisable ... ultimately. From expectations to realities, the pathways were fraught variously, often not in the way we envisage or wished.

The first year was of shock and denial, of suspense, and lack of trust of self. Shock came from it being a very different set-up: its organisation, physical size of the school and student body, a more complex curriculum. It was no longer the 'take (instructions) and deliver (results)' approach, it was 'here is what is available, choose and move', not so gruffly but seemed thoughtless in having the freewill to choose of what one is ignorant or lacked the necessary information: ill-informed and hence misinformed.

The second year was of depression and anger, of gloomy expectancy and fear. An uncertain start in the first carried over to the second with little resolution, groping gingerly, precariously unsettled and indeterminate. Frustration bred depression and some amount of fear. A certain classroom incident of a teacher's misplaced handling of a classmate shook me up, and the ocular short-sightedness that had troubled for nearly two years came to rest when for the first time I requested Pa to acquire a pair of glasses; a self-implanted thorn finally removed. There was an uneasy toilsome difficulty to get 'on the tracks'.

The third year was about hanging on, having reached near bottom in the second, about a rebounding hope and acceptance, of looking forward, with intention to make good and a notion of possibility, the probability of promise, of prospect, of understanding the balance between playing and learning. A discovery that light had always been at the end of the tunnel obscured only by its wide swings in the tortuous journey.

The fourth year was of re-building from a clear sense of purpose, of having turned from lost to purposeful awareness in the second half of secondary three. There was a confidence in having the design of and strategies for a hopeful intended destiny, a seeming likelihood, supposition, of reaching a definite goal, of possibly arriving at the light at the tunnel's end: the unknown elements one could deal with, the devils one could tame; an overwhelming deep assurance restored to push through the gauntlet. Fears overcome, the journey was much cheery, the burden lighter, hopefulness raised, faith renewed and regained.

Expectations have always been real. They have always been realisable . . . ultimately. From expectations to realities, the pathways were fraught variously, often not in the way we envisage or wished. With the appropriate frame and constitution, expectations become realities, regardless of one's station. Expectations are hopes, beliefs, outlook, anticipation, and the trust in their realisation.

Endnotes

Winston Churchill once said, paraphrased here, that ' . . . *failure is not the end . . . success is not final; . . . what matters in failure or success, is the courage to continue'*. His statement was that of a heroic stoic honed in the circumstances around which he was bred, nothing more, nothing less. The stoic is no more than a gutsy human standing on the ground of an unknown faith in the philosophy that virtue is about what one does, that knowledge is attainable through reason. The stoic holds that virtue consists in a will that is in agreement with nature and views self-control and fortitude as means of overcoming supposedly destructive emotions such as anger, jealousy, and envy that are a result of errors in judgment; the virtuous man would be free from such emotions. He is passive to all external events. Such freedom from passion comes from following reason instead of emotions. Today we generally think of stoics as unemotional and steely in the face of suffering and anguish. Brutus, in the Shakespearean play *Julius Caesar* that I studied in secondary four, needlessly died for a cause; as a Roman, he believed devoutly in the stoic principle. I was no stoic, just someone in a confused state seeking to make sense of his uncanny world.

What one does though deemed virtuous may not be necessarily right; the very reason for it may in the first place be flawed. Who decides what is virtuous? Does virtue carry a standard, an absolute unchanging standard? Who makes that standard? Is it flawed man? I cannot imagine he qualifies.

Expectations come at us from within and outside of ourselves: our own construct in historical, cultural, and mental terms, our place in time, our station of birth, the society of men in which we move, the occupation that we adopt or attain, our economic means and ends, our religion, . . . our relative significance as perceived by society at large. Expectations may be born out of our past, who knows. They may be born of those who have a dominant influence in our lives through our obligatory willingness, or a sweeping adoration of their persona. Do we explore the roots of our expectations sufficiently to realise they may not be ours? When we come to them, it would be no surprise that they change, that they may be at odds with our deepest beliefs, that congruence is not bound. They are all borne with imperfections, with impermanence, characteristic of the world we live in. we cannot experience *the peace that passes all understanding*. We long for perfect peace; wherefore our expectation must be from our Creator and not from ourselves relative to the world about us. *My soul, wait thou only upon God; for my expectation is from him.*—Psalm 62:5.

3

At Thirteen — Shock and Denial, Lost

I have gone astray like a lost sheep . . . .
—Psalm 119:176

My first year at RI was a blur; I was in 'dream' mode, trying to settle in, to understand what worked, and what did not. I learned that one must lead otherwise one would be led. My early years and religious inclinations did not prepare for me to lead, I was more a team member who merged in with the group, who interfaced and blended well with others where one does well and be asked to lead. I was not comfortable with self-appointed high visibility leadership.

The broad choices for core extra-curricular activities (ECA) were there, the information without the experiential content was of little value, the time to decide was inadequate when one's plate was full. One had to make the decision and stick with it for the next four years or more. I chose to join the school band because I wanted to play the trumpet for all its imagined glamour and at the same time to learn music that we could ill afford on a paying and private basis. I was to receive a shock when my request for trumpet position did not materialise because my decision was late in coming and the demand from those wanting to learn the trumpet was overwhelming. Over the years, the school band became my pre-occupation, consumed much of my time, and was well worth the investment; in the third year, I received appointment to the first trumpet position when the bandmaster discovered my skill, and my secret training efforts paid off.

My assignment to class 1E had no significance attached: I believed it was a random allocation based probably on the schools from which we came. The only other boy from Jervois East was with me at 1E. A group of five students were all from Outram Primary, and similarly with others. Only in the second year, students with better results in the first year went to the better class beginning with 'A' and through to 'H', the worst performing students went to 'H'. The secondary ones, twos, and threes were in the afternoon session; secondary fours along with pre-university ones and twos were in the morning.

The sense of being lost was a recurring theme for the first two years at RI. There was the feeling of no longer possessing or retaining the abilities that made entry to RI possible in the first place, a sense of struggle in hanging on to them. With the struggle, there was the fear of wasted and lost opportunities, hence a prodigal loss of time. It was as going astray, losing direction, missing the way with no help or guide at hand. I felt disoriented, confused, puzzled, bemused, perplexed, and bewildered as to place and direction.

3.1 Softball and Cross-country

Softball is a variant of American baseball. In fact, there are two types of softball, the slow pitch, and the fast pitch. The slow pitch was not a school sport. I remembered we played it as a 'loose-in-rules' game called 'rounders'. At RI, fast pitch softball played out in the open field with nine players on each team: catcher, pitcher, and shortstop; first, second, and third basemen; left, centre, and right outfielders. The pitching was an underhand pitch, fast but slower than the American baseball pitch. It was the first sport I tried my hand at on the urging of my school mate at Jervois East who entered RI with me. I knew nothing about it nor the status of our 'trial' training on the side, and wasted several months joining and accompanying him in the morning, Mie packing sandwiches filled with onions fried in eggs for me to take along as brunch. We were throwing and catching balls, and did some batting that would never get us anywhere near to joining the school team. We were both of small stature, and making no sense of it I gave it up after three months as wishful thinking of my friend. I learned never to tangle with a pursuit that I had absolutely no interest in and had no clear end in view. It was a sheer childish folly formed of a whim, a caprice. A lesson learnt early was a useful marker for life, to hold close as a reminder in future encounters of the same sort.

Cross-country was meaningful. I volunteered to represent the team for my age grouping in Hullett House, one of the five Houses (Moor, Morrison, Bayley, and Buckley). Voluntarism meant nothing unless one meets the minimum requirements. Hullett was my given House for all the time in RI. We had trials to time our runs at the school field and another at MacRitchie Reservoir also a nature reserve, where the annual cross-country runs took place. My time was good to be included in the Hullett team after trial runs at school. I had never run a cross-country race and did not quite know what to expect. Running in the field and around the school buildings was easy enough as they were a familiar sight where I knew what to expect of the terrain, placement, and so on. I was familiar with the elements and could pace myself accordingly. However, the second trial exposed me to the real thing. We met at the meeting place where the memorial of a past personality was, were then given instructions on the route, received our tags to be pinned on the singlet, and off we went into the run. I wore my ordinary China-made thin-soled white canvas shoes, the same ones that took me to and from school daily. They were the ones I have always had, and have been used to. After the run through the MacRitchie reserve, I realised the shoes would not take the strain if one trained regularly: it lacked the grip to my feet, did not hold well to sloping sections of the terrain, and the sole simply too thin to cushion the impact of sudden drops. Overall the shoes stressed the sole, ankle, and the whole leg. Still, it was manageable. The terrain took me by surprise: the near-dried smooth mudflats proved slippery sometimes; the mildly undulating terrain created sudden drops and raises that interrupted the rhythm. The windings required watchfulness, intermittent little pools of collected rainwater waiting not to be disturbed, the overhanging branches of trees got in the way occasionally, blinding streaks of sunlight penetrating through the tall trees making it difficult to see through the shadows. The air was musty, at some points dank. All one saw was the runners in front within twenty five metres on a straight stretch. The second part of the run was easier under open skies along the mostly straight occasionally gently-curved Lornie Road and back to the starting point at the reservoir. I ran and came in with the middle of the pack. When unable to mass with the front pack, the trick was to join the middle group and keep with it to the finish line to clock a respectable time. I was one runner who had no clue what a good time was. My job was to end well, not necessarily at the top and certainly not at the bottom. It was interesting and with more practice to gain familiarity with the nuances of the terrain and elements within the Reserve, one could run a reasonably good race. I did not attend any other practices at MacRitchie and ran the finals on another day. We only had occasional practices around the school compound. MacRitchie was far from home and time was scarce. Again, the cross-country race was not like a run of my life: I was available. I met the trial times which meant I qualified as a runner. I collected ECA points, gained the experience of running in one, and it did not absorb an undue amount of practice hours. It was the only one such cross-country race that I participated at House level in all my years at RI.

I was equipped with sword and shield whose efficacy I have begun to question. Hemmed in I was; lost, I continued in darkness.

3.2 School Band & Music—Euphonium

I chose to join the band to learn music, as I had never had the opportunity before; no tuition charged, the musical instrument was a free loan . . . how wonderful. In a short time of joining the band I realised there was very little teaching of music, I had to learn it all on my own. The senior instrumentalist trained new entrants to read music scores, the notes, the rests, expressions, and so on, enough to play the instrument to produce the note on the score in unison with others. It was as an older brother showing the younger the ropes. I was grateful the older brothers were themselves reasonably respectable musicians in the band with keen personal interest in music. In the beginning, attempts at coordinating the pace of score sight-reading with playing/blowing the instrument were disastrous. We were not proficient in the use of the instrument—a case of 'new' lips—and in our ability to effectively read musical scores in keeping with the bandmaster's baton. When we were more familiar with our instruments, more in control of the sounds and tones we produced, only then did it all come together, synchronised, and sensible. That took a good full year to achieve. There was a struggle in learning and I had to learn through discovery. After band training on Saturdays, I usually borrowed the instrument home to practice. The euphonium in a hard case was quite unwieldy, a cumbersome travel burden that stood at about two-thirds my height, and quite heavy for someone such as me who was of little build and stature. I looked clumsy, a little of out of place, possibly weird. Stoically, I trudged on, sometimes feeling silly in a bus and on occasions a little proud to be a 'musician'. It would have felt better if I was carrying a trumpet case. The good thing was that buses were less crowded on Saturdays. Boosey & Hawkes in England manufactured these brass instruments, with the 'Sovereign' imprint engraved on the outside of the instruments' bells.

The euphonium is a conical-bore, tenor-voiced brass instrument. It produces a 'well-sounding' or 'sweet-voiced' rounded tone. The euphonium is a valved instrument, piston valved. The person playing it is an *euphonist*. As with the other conical-bore instruments, the euphonium's tubing gradually increases in diameter throughout its length, resulting in a softer, gentler tone compared to other cylindrical-bore instruments such as the trumpet, trombone, and baritone. The characteristic euphonium sound is 'cuddly'—snugly rich, round, warm, and velvety—with virtually no hardness to it. The hold of it was also cuddly as in kissing a dance partner, with the left hand wrapped around her body with no legs and the right hand fingering the three valves as in clasping her left hand.

The instrument I badly wanted to learn and play at was the trumpet, for no other reason than that I have seen and heard of its sound most often, that it stood out among all the other brass instruments. Its loftiness and distinguished quality of tone, and the bright loud sound produced made everyone desire it; I missed the first-come-first-served cut and had to settle for the euphonium. The trumpet is the instrument with the highest register in the brass family and stood out clearly. It played by blowing air through closed lips, producing a 'buzzing' sound to start a standing wave vibration in the air column inside the instrument. Much of the sound produced is controlled by the lips. The trumpet is a length of brass tubing, bent twice into a rounded oblong shape and has three piston valves. Each valve increases the length of tubing when engaged, thereby lowering the pitch.

The school band became an important cornerstone in my school life. It was an endeavour pursued with much passion against steep but common odds. It epitomised the principle that to what I laid my hand, I must pursue ardently, and bring it to completion. In a sense, there was this driven need to be responsible for the expected outcome. Oftentimes, that meant *not waiting for things to happen* but to actively engage in *making things happen.* In the natural law of things, this is all well, just *cause-and—effect* reaping what one sows. The action causes the results one can reasonably expect and outcomes one can knowingly foresee; it cannot say or know beyond that. Only our Maker can. *Seest thou a man diligent in his business? He shall stand before kings; he shall not stand before mean men.*—Proverbs 22:29.

3.3 Poetry and Shane—First Taste of English Literature

Shane, a novel by Jack Schaeffer first published in 1901, and An Anthology of Poems whose editor I simply had not etched in my memory. These two books made up our study texts for the English Literature subject. Shane was a Western story about a drifter and retired gunfighter or gunslinger who assists a homestead family terrorised by an ageing cattleman and his hired gun. Schaeffer did not indicate whether Shane was a hired gunfighter and if so, what sort of a hired gunfighter had he been. The book opened our eyes to analysis of the storyline, of the writer's skill in narrative, in using observation/study of human expressions, effects of the happenings, and so on to portray the message without directly telling us about it. This was our first forays into what literature was seemingly about. There was no definite morals discussed; it was like the accepted standard version of the good versus the bad, the just versus the unjust, and their merited reward or deserving retribution. In looking back, it was best to have left them alone without further discussion; I can now see difficulties in interpretation even at our age then. The story had many questions left unanswered for a young person, our understanding and knowledge of right and wrong had not quite developed to a meaningful point. There was no need for that then.

As an adult, I can now see a whole multitude of contentious questions about principles, morals, and relationships. It can be rather complex compared to the individual and serial books Enid Blyton wrote for us kids: Secret Seven, and adventures of the Famous Five. Fiction after the age of innocence never quite caught my fancy; those that I have seriously read probably counted less than the fingers on my one hand. Nevertheless, literature allowed us to look beyond the story to consider human nature in its higher and baser motives, not to critique, opine about or compare. Shane passed into the distance quietly, a wounded victor, an oblivious benefactor. His place was not among the homesteaders. Was the wound fatal? Whatever happened to him beyond the book forever hung over our heads. That leaves an opportunity for Shane—The Return!

Poetry did not make much sense to me, why should the poet write in a manner so non-literal that we needed analytical studies on his poems. I would never know why he wrote the way he did, I have no means of understanding his life's background, or analysing his mental state at the time he wrote it. It was as though we were involved in something that was of little interest to us other than a frivolous meddling of the poet's privacy in that our analysis could end up totally wrong. Who can know it? Finally, I was ready to believe it was all about style in powerfully conjuring up thoughts and emotions in a language subtle and obscure as to be mystical in the use of metaphors and imagery. We studied several great poems that were straightforward and simple, with lines that rhymed, with verses that caused the poem to 'sing', bring on the 'theatrics' and say what they wanted to say. Some were clearly humorous short of hilarious. The book was *An Anthology* and we were required to study selected ones, I cursorily browsed through the others for personal enjoyment. An anthology being a collection of poems by different poets from different ages, was, I thought a good thing to start out with. It offered a young novice an appreciation of the different styles as well as an opportunity to explore our preferences. Some poems can be dark and gloomy, some simply comical and fun, some heroic, others are standalone depiction of an historic event, an epic such as Lord Byron's poem that was about the destruction of the army of Sennacherib who took up a campaign against King Hezekiah of Judah in attempt to lay siege of Jerusalem. This account was Biblical (2 Kings 18-19). I was too uninterested about all things Christian in those days and had not noted any Biblical connections, and if the teacher had mentioned anything of that sort it must have completely missed my ears. *And it came to pass that night, that the angel of the LORD went out, and smote in the camp of the Assyrians an hundred fourscore and five thousand: and when they arose early in the morning, behold, they were all dead corpses.*—2 Kings 19:35. This poem was quite remarkable in that if one were to read with rhythm like in a march, one could really feel the 'music' as in a war movie. You may try it here with the verses below.

The Assyrian came down like the wolf on the fold,
And his cohorts were gleaming in purple and gold;
And the sheen of their spears was like stars on the sea,
When the blue wave rolls nightly on deep Galilee.

Like the leaves of the forest when Summer is green,
That host with their banners at sunset were seen:
Like the leaves of the forest when Autumn hath blown,
That host on the morrow lay withered and strown.

For the Angel of Death spread his wings on the blast,
And breathed in the face of the foe as he passed;
And the eyes of the sleepers waxed deadly and chill,
And their hearts but once heaved, and for ever grew still!

And there lay the steed with his nostril all wide,
But through it there rolled not the breath of his pride;

And the foam of his gasping lay white on the turf,
And cold as the spray of the rock-beating surf.

And there lay the rider distorted and pale,
With the dew on his brow, and the rust on his mail:
And the tents were all silent, the banners alone,
The lances unlifted, the trumpet unblown.

And the widows of Ashur are loud in their wail,
And the idols are broke in the temple of Baal;
And the might of the Gentile, unsmote by the sword,
Hath melted like snow in the glance of the Lord.

Wilfred Owen was heralded as a leading First World War poet whose poems I thought could be better appreciated with some knowledge and experience of the horrors of trench warfare, not only the physical conditions that threw up a myriad of emotions, but also the loneliness, uncertainty of life, and the purposelessness of war. During my National Service in later years, I had a taste of that but it was really mild in that it was about the methods and approaches in a training scenario not stretched out over months and years as in a prolonged war. It was certainly highly claustrophobic, the narrow trenches and network of them on a hill made us feel like rats in a tight maze with every move a hazard as we scratched or tore against barb wires and stinting iron pickets. Zinc sheets to hold back falling earth and retained by iron pickets each a metre apart was the only saving friendly surface that trained our bodies to move in rhythm to avoid hurt.

Endnotes
Poetry and classic prose have their place in our modern world where people communicate more directly as in a transaction, and perhaps too briefly to bring enough feelings and the value of those powerful emotions to

bear on a matter deserving of more rounded and fuller meaning. Poetry has the capability of bringing on the highs, creating a terseness that compacts as weighty, slicing through the mirrors and shadows, revealing truth in mere conversations. Our communication has become transactional, to convey a defined purpose and little beyond; it has become displaced with laughing, joking and jiving, spewing frivolous inanities, parroting the commonplace, uttering the politically correct; leaving the bosom of sincere feeling and thoughtfulness in another realm. Silence seems difficult to bear as an unspoken language, supposedly a paradoxical vehicle of thought. We have become mere receiving and transmitting stations.

What is life's purpose? How will study, as a participant of the education system lead us to that purpose? How will the study of characters in literature contribute to an understanding of life's purpose? Unless we know the answer to the very first question, we cannot reckon it. We have to look to the Son of God in His lowliness and humility in obedience to His Father's will to be the only suitable sacrificial Son of man. In the moment of our belief in the Son of God, we have faith in His efficacy for our salvation from God's wrath; we . . . *should not perish but have everlasting life*. Christ is our everlasting anchor. God loves the world, the whole world, all of mankind . . . to whosoever that believes in Him, the promise of everlasting life. *And further, by these, my son, be admonished: of making many books there is no end; and much study is a weariness of the flesh.*—Ecclesiastes 12:12

3.4 Perry Mason, the Defenders, and Law

Perry Mason was an American legal drama where the episodes discovered the guilty party without actually going to trial. At the preliminary hearing, the district attorney needed only to produce enough evidence to convince the judge that the defendant should go to trial. Mason's tough, relentless, and clever questioning of other culprits or criminal accomplices forced them into confessions, and exposed the real killer.

The Defenders is an American courtroom drama series that ran on CBS from 1961-1965. It starred E. G. Marshall and Robert Reed as father-and-son defence lawyers who specialized in legally complex cases that I had little memory of, my attention was on the legal process, and the manner of argument.

In both these legal dramas, my key interest was in the court arguments, and the way evidence applied to them. What also attracted me were the colourful speaking abilities of Perry Mason, and E. G. Marshall and his son. There was a time I was motivated to be a lawyer and Mie said I could be one because I would often take a point of discussion, question it, and convincingly positioned it against hers. We both did not know what the law profession entailed; it was all merely banter between us. We should have known better than to apply legal techniques at home where Mother's Law prevailed. A further TV serial movie, *The Paper Chase* that I watched during the seventies about law school at Harvard continued my lifetime interest in law. In this movie, the law professor Charles Kingsfield was most intimidating and his student Mr. Hart was responsively impressive in standing to him in areas of law. *The Paper Chase* was different from Perry Mason and The Defenders in that it offered a further discussion in matters of law, drawing out the fine distinction of rights and obligations in the governance of equity as defined by the rule of law. It paved the way for a continuing romance with the legal profession.

Endnotes

After every viewing of those movies, there were things that bothered the mind: who decided how the law should be? How does the lawmaker know what would be right or wrong? Can a king or appointed power turn the law on its head? Was not brute force greater than the law? A coup d'état knows no law? A rape victim can only identify the rapist and puts him behind bars. Is that redress? Can the violation be undone? These were just questions . . . for one too young to know enough about too little.

The law was certainly not perfect and in many instances powerless; it served only as *deterrence* to the violator but not necessarily deterred; to the violated, no recompense where an eye for eye became time in jail for an eye. For the dastardly care-less, offensive deterred, the deterrent loses its teeth, and the law goes out the window. Today, the emphasis is *compliance*.

The shifting sands of time: deterrence suggests possible transgression, compliance suggests possible violation, and they deal similarly. Deterrence suggests painful consequences for violation, and more direct. Compliance suggests correction for deviation from institutionalised methods.

Now, however, do we ever need the law of the world, the law written by man, changed by man to adapt to changing times, their values and mores? Is that even law if it changes with the whims of an imperfect world? Did not God the perfect Lawgiver give us an immaculate law to unreservedly obey? *And the LORD God commanded the man, saying, of every tree of the garden thou mayest freely eat: But of the tree of the knowledge of good and evil, thou shalt not eat of it: for in the day that thou eatest thereof thou shalt surely die.*—Genesis 2:16-17.

We have failed laws, imperfect ones that came from a corrupt world of denigrated man. Man flouted and suffered the consequence. Sin has no hedge, no garrison around it. Breaking the law is in man's blood hence man enacted more laws with circumspection of the circumvention of laws. Only one law stands out for all eternity: *For God so loved the world, that he gave his only begotten Son, that whosoever believeth in him should not perish, but have everlasting life.*—John 3:16. *For the law was given by Moses, but grace and truth came by Jesus Christ.*—John 1:17.

3.5 My sight—Art

In the secondary one Art examination, the subject tested was Still Life. Several objects displayed on a writing desk draped over in white cloth, in front of the class. The objects included a tennis ball can with a cap over the top, a tennis ball alongside it on the outside that allowed its shape to highlight the shadow that fell on the white table cloth and effects on its curves, and a tennis racquet positioned at an angle to heighten the perspective thrown by its length. All looked well and comfortable for my understanding, however, my bad eyesight could not make out the words on the container, and that bothered me. After some consideration, I raised my hand and the teacher came by my desk to enquire of my request. He allowed me to go to the front for a close up view of the wordings on the can. I memorised the key wordings, went back to my seat to finish up my sketch, and completed the painting for submission. The eye test at Jervois East showed I needed a pair of spectacles if not soon. This time, I realised my eyes were not well. Still I decided not to tell Pa about it until I had serious trouble with them. I received a credit for Art. I never really got around to an understanding of art, it was a subject we had in the first two years at RI after which we went on to the science stream and very much left it. There was little about an appreciation of art, it was mostly about a brief explanation followed by sketching and colouring over with pastels or painting over with water/poster colours. I rather liked to paint from real objects in great positions that brought out the perspectives, direction of light and casting of shadows. Imaginary scenes were difficult for me, I was unable to hold a scene in my mind for long enough to pin it down to sketch, and even if I could, I had trouble anchoring its shape and colours. Perhaps imagination was unreal and my brain had made up its mind to shutout the unreal or the practical had been pervasive in my experiences. Still life fitted in well with me or me with it.

Visual arts in painting and drawing/sketching as a part of my education truly offered a pleasant diversion; it was enjoyable, I had an innate inclination to it, less of an appreciation of it, and a certain introductory ability with both the pencil and the brush, of charcoal and water colours. Art was as a luxury in my education. It took time to think and plan about a piece of work, and time was preciously scarce. The high-B pencils and special erasers were costly and paints priced dearly, the paper required sometimes thicker than the normal; I was keenly aware and stinting in their use for want of the budget. Whenever at the school library and as the opportunity presents, I would browse books of drawings and paintings by artists of time past, along with those on general knowledge. In later years, I saved up enough pocket money to buy a little book about sketching with related techniques to apply in different dynamics; it was a worthwhile investment.

Endnotes

Years later as an adult, I would watch the potter at his art, and attended an eleven week course on Chinese calligraphy. These were times of exhilaration in understanding scriptural use of the 'potter and the clay', and consider God 'painting' the heaven and the earth into being. Every brush stroke in Chinese calligraphy is a stroke of perfection that man can attempt to achieve but knowing it to be impossible. The love, the understanding that bears on the hand to exert gradations of pressure on the brush hairs, or to lift them in paces and strengths, draw out the beauty of every stroke: vertical, horizontal, upstroke, down-stroke, lift, tail, jot, and tittle. The hand, manifests the caring understanding character of the calligrapher, collaborates with the ink, the rice paper, and the property of the brush with its soft, willing, and meek goat hairs on the outside of the brush mop that wraps around the stiffer stubborn wolf hairs in the centre stem of the brush. This bears for us the reminder of the Creator's gentle care in His correction, His crying tenderness when He allows severe painful affliction to come upon us. Yet His holiness and righteousness hold fast and unyielding. Every stroke drives the calligrapher's breath. Learning the art gives one a sense of God's great care for His creation in tenderness and forcefulness, in pushing and in lifting, in anger and in pleasure, in tarrying and in driving forth, in starkness and in splendour, in lightness and in gravity. *God gives us time and opportunity to consider the works of artists, of mortal man that we may consider the works of His hand in the expansive eternal canvas of His creation. He grants us time to 'stand and stare' at the flowers, smell the verdure, fly with the flitting yellow butterflies . . . to immerse in the beauty His hand has wrought. Artists paint from His rocks, hills, and trees; His skies, His time and seasons, His seas, the rustling grass, the carolling birds, the faces/portraits of man, woman, and child . . . He made them all marvellously and wonderfully. He fills in every line, furrow, and crease: the details the artist misses in the forlorn, the lonely, the fearful, the innocent, and the worried. On the obverse He takes pleasure in the ecstasy, the joyful, the comforted, the playful, the contented, and the grateful. He understands the deepest thoughts of a face, of the emotion in a smile, a frown; the tilt of a head, the look in the eyes, placement of the fingers, the hands . . . that the artist customarily sees on the skin. He colours His creation in shades to manifest His purpose that the artist can only concoct in limited degrees. He is simply awesome, breath-taking!*

Here is what hymn writer Maltbie Babcock tells us about My Father's World, God's World.

This is my Father's world, And to my list'ning ears,
All nature sings, and round me rings The music of the spheres.
This is my Father's world, I rest me in the thought
Of rocks and trees, of skies and seas;
His hand the wonders wrought.

This is my Father's world, The birds their carols raise;
The morning light, the lily white Declare their Maker's praise.
This is my Father's world, He shines in all that's fair;
In the rustling grass I hear Him pass,
He speaks to me ev'rywhere.

This is my Father's world, O let me ne'er forget
That though the wrong seems oft so strong, God is the Ruler yet.
This is my Father's world, The battle is not done;
Jesus who died shall be satisfied,
And earth and heav'n be one.

When I consider thy heavens, the work of thy fingers, the moon and the stars, which thou hast ordained; what is man, that thou art mindful of him? And the son of man, that thou visitest him? For thou hast made him a little lower than the angels, and hast crowned him with glory and honour. Thou madest him to have dominion over the works of thy hands; thou hast put all things under his feet: all sheep and oxen, yea, and the beasts of the field; the fowl of the air, and the fish of the sea, and whatsoever passeth through the paths of the seas. O LORD our Lord, how excellent is thy name in all the earth!—Psalm 8:3-9.

3.6 Bahasa Kebangsaan still around

Bahasa Kebangsaan (BK), our national language in Malay was still around except it was now not an examinable subject. There were no grades given. We attended class: the teacher got someone to read aloud from the text, explained some words, and wrote out some homework for us to do. There was little or no pressure to learning. This was clearly farcical and little wonder that students of my time missed learning Malay altogether. The subject slid into the curriculum invisibly, no one knew what it was, and none cared. Easily learned, it used the English alphabet to concoct its sound: romanised Malay. Wasteful it was! Over the next few years, it disappeared totally from the curriculum.

We acquire language through social interaction in early childhood, when as children we speak fluently at about three years old. The use of language is entrenched in our culture for communicative and social, and cultural uses, to signify group/racial identity, social layering, and in some cases, for entertainment. Our people had not found BK useful other than the few words for greetings ('selamat pagi' for good morning), numbers to help with transaction ('tiga puloh' for thirty), agreement/ disagreement ('boleh' for can, 'tak boleh' for cannot) and so on. Each of those situations before mentioned were direct usages. When one needed to include more dimensions to elaborate and explain, BK cannot go further: the non-Malay users did not have the vocabulary, nor the grammar, structural constructs to even begin. It was then back to the use of English if the person communicated to had some usable knowledge of it. Young children not taught forcefully on its use, makes the effort at a later age quite a gargantuan task.

The immigrant Chinese race was of greater numbers and used more of its native language and dialects than the indigent language. Integration into the indigent culture and language was difficult. There was little need to, and with the competing call for English as the first language in the face of national economic aspirations, Bahasa Kebangsaan in Malay was naturally and silently unfitting. Chinese walked the same path and went to school with little or no enthusiasm. Bahasa Kebangsaan met its natural demise. In later years when we watched a potentially vibrant China rise upon the world economic stage, opening its doors to world trade, Chinese was vigorously promoted—the adaptation of a small fry in the ocean of changing tides. Adoption that is dependent on needs is culturally non-progressive and may prove destructive in the long run, merely treated as an *opportunistic* means to a *mercenary* end. Hollow adoption of practices in the name of tradition can only bear the fruit of ceremonial superficiality.

And he said unto them, Full well ye reject the commandment of God, that ye may keep your own tradition.—Mark 7:9. . . . *making the word of God of none effect through your tradition, which ye have delivered: and many such like things do ye.*—Mark 7:13. *Beware lest any man spoil you through philosophy and vain deceit, after the tradition of men, after the rudiments of the world, and not after Christ.*—Colossians 2:8

3.7 Mah-jong

Mah-jong was a table game for four players, one with which my family was familiar. There were 136 tiles bearing Chinese characters, bamboo, and circles each numbering 1 through 9. Each number had 4 matching tiles. One honour suit had winds from different directions: east, north, west, south. The other suit had 3 tiles: red (Chinese character of 'centre'), green (Chinese character of 'grow' or 'prosper'), and white (a rectangular coloured frame). All the suits had 4 tiles of each. There is a lot more to say about the game but for our purpose, the aforementioned is sufficient for your understanding.

It first started out as a past-time, Mie playing with the older ladies next door, and on the third floor. Their friends joined in on occasions. It was usually for the afternoon to occupy housewives in their day's lull and for old folks to exercise their mental agility. It was a game of skill, strategy, and calculation of the tiles exposed and those still in the hands or in the undrawn decks: not particularly complex but adequately intelligent. Pa was away at work. Pa was very good in counting and guessing whether he should hold on to a tile. Skill sometimes may not let one win the game. It only pre-empted blatant errors that could affect one's own game or carelessly frustrate that of others. There was a need to understand the inter-relationships and interdependencies. It was quite an intelligent game though not with any high degree of complexity due to the limited permutations from a small number of tiles per suit and featured suits.

There was a certain discipline about playing the game in its early days when the game promptly wrapped up at five in the afternoon so that Mie and the others could go home and prepare dinners for their families. During the school breaks whenever I was around at home, Mie would allow me to take her hand at mah-jong while she went to prepare dinner. This was occasional but I learned to be quite good at it after a while.

After some while, mah-jong became a fixed routine, a habit, and with other intrusions, it became a little less than gambling for the low stakes. It was not a serious game both on the side of recreation as well as on the side of gambling. Mah-jong had quite an influence in our lives for a short stretch of a few years and a sharing of that would throw some light on its effects. Pa and Mie became acquainted with an educated and decent married couple at the temple. They were well-dressed and often rode on a scooter to the temple. After a little time, they visited us regularly and became close friends of our family. Not long after, playing the mah-jong on weekend nights became a regular thing when all parties had no work and were available. If it was on a Saturday night, the sessions ran over into the wee hours of Sunday. On Sundays, they and others would play from the early afternoon until about a little past dinner time. This became a change in our lives: it was noisy when the mah-jong got 'washed' (mixed up) by the eight hands to even the odds before stacking them up, all facing down, and throwing dices to decide who would take the first stack of four pieces. When playing, it became natural for the men to smoke cigarettes. The smoke-filled living hall was a place to avoid for we all, the children, had an abhorrence for smoke; we had an aversion to smoke. When a light draught was about and the smoke wafted into our bedroom where we were poring over our books, we had to take a light cardboard to fan away the smoke. The smoke affected our concentration; we could ignore the sounds of mah-jong but was helpless against the dissipating smoke that stole into our noses and choked our minds. Occasionally, out of frustration, I took a break and watched them play with my cardboard fanning about my nose making it known we were troubled by the smoking. My observation had been in that many hours of playing, they were completely engrossed with gaining the upper hand against each other, leaving all other thoughts aside. In the early stretches of the game, the air was typically lively, players chatted easily, discussing the news, some amount of gossiping, sharing experiences with much excitement, and in brighter intonations. As the game wore on, the conversations thinned out, became scant, monologues turned on, voices flat, in monotones, as though boredom and fatigue took over. One person muttered incoherence, no one else responded to, and everyone dulled and numbed. All else became an inconspicuous low drone. As mah-jong was supposedly a past-time, the stakes were small. It was certainly an odd way to pass the time. Life was much like that: as initial objectives changed, the transacting relationships adjust in response, causing the moods to alter.

Endnotes

The scenes at mah-jong bring to mind those I saw at a pachinko bar in downtown Tokyo when I visited one of the regional offices in Japan as a senior company executive. Pachinko is a vertical pinball game machine where the player earns balls that they exchange for non-cash prizes. There were just endless neat rows of pachinko machines and the typical Japanese male office staff would after dinner sit at these machines, eyes half-closed, one hand working the machine as though they knew the machines better than their wives. There was an absolute sense of walking into a zombie hall of males hardly moving, at their pachinko machines. The men were just bored to death with pinballs going *chink-chink-chink*. It was traditional practice and expectation for the men, the family bread winners to not return home early as though they were at work till late. They headed for the pachinko bars for some hours before they made their way home at the acceptable hour.

Gaming, on the continuum from recreation to gambling means all the same: a prodigal waste of time, an abuse in the use of time, a dampener on the mental faculties, an attendance to idolatry, a drain on financial resources, a stealthy acceptance of chance in life and encounters of life. *The lot is cast into the lap; but the whole disposing thereof is of the LORD.*—Proverbs 16:33

3.8 Changing Neighbourhood

At home, our neighbourhood had undergone change. Next to our SIT (Singapore Improvement Trust, precursor of HDB) flats, new HDB eighteen-storey rental flats have sprouted to provide housing to the lower income families. They were essentially one-room flats much like what we now know as studio apartments. Every level in each block of flats had a common corridor that separates the housing units. A main door opened into the unit's dining or living area depending on how the lessee wished to organise it. On its left is a long hall way that was the bedroom with a window at the far end, and to its front was an access to the tiny 2-stove kitchen, and further front was the balcony with the washroom to its right. Generally, it was adequately decent for a family of two adults and perhaps two small children at the most. The design was Spartan in that the floors had a layer of screed and offered the lessee the flexibility of tiling them over or laying them with linoleum or rolled mats. The lessee could also create one or two unauthorised separators to delineate the bedroom area, and the dining/living area. Some families used drawn curtains as separators or standing cabinets to mark the separation. You may remember in the earlier book, *Age of Innocence*, that GGA (great grand aunt) and Aunt shared a unit in one of these eighteen-storey blocks. So the tenants were not just from the lower income groups but included the older folks without immediate families to care for them. With the lower income families moving into these flats in quite large numbers, our peaceful neighbourhood turned on its head. It had become very unsettling with clamour from the slamming of doors and of shouting from family squabbles within the households and from disagreements between households. Gambling in little temporary open stalls made their presence and created gambling dens of sorts. With them came personal and gang fights and robberies, police patrols often made their rounds, and summoned into the area particularly in the evenings. The neighbourhood was no longer safe for young girls and women to traverse the streets without escort. It

49

reminded me of the Kampong Silat area where the Thai Buddhist temple was situated. Perhaps that was how the ghettos around the world came to be.

It brings to mind a Chinese lesson taught when in school about Mencius' mother moving house three times to find the right environment to raise her son. Mencius was a Confucian scholar and his mother's diligence paid off, hence the Chinese saying 'Mencius' mother's three moves'. Mencius's father died when he was very young. His mother raised him alone. They were very poor. They *first* lived next to a cemetery, where Mencius imitated the paid mourners in funeral processions. His mother thought this to be inappropriate for her growing son. Their *second* move was to a house near a market in the town. Mencius began to imitate the cries of peddlers (classified as lowly and despised in those days). His mother's *third* and final move was to a house next to a school. Imitating the scholars and students, Mencius studied and became a scholar. He established himself as one among China's greatest moral teachers and philosophers.

Although we were not much involved with the neighbourhood, it was quite unsettling when we hear the breaking of beer bottles, or some belligerent cries and shouts in the air. The sirens of patrol cars, the roaring motorcycles, the screeching of brakes stopped our hearts often, and disturbed the pleasant settings we once enjoyed. Time and the lack of alternatives eased us into the neighbourhood as we became accustomed to its noises and moods, became familiar with what to expect, to avoid, and to stay clear. We could become a part of the environment but our upbringing grounded in Buddhist fundamentals as well as the family mandate set a hedge between us.

Blessed is the man who walks not in the counsel of the wicked, nor stands in the way of sinners, nor sits in the seat of scoffers; but his delight is in the law of the LORD, and on his law he meditates day and night. He is like a tree planted by streams of water that yields its fruit in its season, and its leaf does not wither. In all that he does, he prospers.—Psalm 1:1-3.

3.9 Bethesda chapel

Christian classmates continually invited others and me, to Bethesda Chapel along Bras Basah Road before class begun on Tuesday. The intention was clear: to convert non-believers. We were all well aware of the intentions but went along just to satisfy our curiosity. We have never been inside a church, and had watched movies where the churches in small and poor Western/Mexican town were Roman Catholic with simple straight white walls both inside and outside of them often led at the altar by a simple-frocked *padre*. The pew benches were jointing of simple wood pieces. The large opulent high-ceilinged churches seen mostly in English/European period movies had the priest elaborately dressed in white and gold with tall head dress servicing an equally ornate altar. Bethesda was a little better than the poor Western/Mexican church, simple single-storey small church, with nothing that one could class as elaborate. The preacher wore shirt and pants like common folk. I recall nothing of the message preached and was more interested in the formality and manner of the service conducted. There was a certain peace and quiet during the service, a reverential feeling of comfort where all hustle and bustle shut out for the duration of it. *As it was a Christian worship service, we did not ask the many questions on our minds.*

Endnotes

Who is God? Why is there a God? Where is He? Why are there problems in the world? Where is God in these problems? Why should I believe in Him? Who created the world? What evidences exist to prove? Why should I be sinful just because Adam was sinful? Much of which was mere derision of my Christian friends who were themselves young in the Christian faith, lacking the necessary training to handle and address such matters, thereby setting forth unconvincing statements, arguments that only projected themselves as weak, common, reactive defences. We easily turned down and rejected their untenable positions. It was simply saying they have proven themselves unable to prove that which they set out to prove, or to disprove that which atheists and sceptics have in their bosoms. The former cannot hold for the Word of God is God's authority, it was in the beginning, sure and objective. The latter was pointless for atheism and scepticism rested on little more than unbelief and preference, highly subjective in nature.

It is strange that most of the time when a religion presented to us is other than our own, we go on the offence, and build up a wall brick by brick as each statement or argument blunted against thick resistance. There were times we listened passively and with disinterest, justly rude, and stonewalling. Religious conversion of man at man's own level of understanding must perpetually be a disaster given his dark human condition, his human resistance to change. Seeking solutions at a level higher than man can truly purport to be the viable agent of change in man.

The task was to hold the ground in what we professed, in a religion (Buddhism) that now stood on loosening earth as we faced the realities of knowledge, understanding, and reason. Early faith in Buddhism, founded on familial profession was beginning to fade in the face of competing, contending essence and acceptance. Yet I clung on tenaciously to Buddhism because Pa was Buddhist and as though that my role as son was to perpetuate it. There was a rising sense of difficulty in reconciling my childhood with the wider complex world that lay in the foreground to be conquered. How am I to do that? I was equipped with sword and shield whose efficacy I have begun to question. Hemmed in, I was; lost, I continued in darkness. *But sanctify the Lord God in your hearts: and be ready always to give an answer to every man that asketh you a reason of the hope that is in you with meekness and fear:*—1 Peter 3:15. *Study to shew thyself approved unto God, a workman that needeth not to be ashamed, rightly dividing the word of truth.*—2 Timothy 2:15. *They shall speak of the glory of thy kingdom, and talk of thy power; to make known to the sons of men his mighty acts, and the glorious majesty of his kingdom.*—Psalm 145:11-12.

. . . The heavens declare the glory of God; and the firmament sheweth his handywork. Psalms 19:1

The fool says in his heart, "There is no God." They are corrupt, they do abominable deeds, there is none who does good. The LORD looks down from heaven on the children of man, to see if there are any who understand, who seek after God. They have all turned aside; together they have become corrupt; there is none who does good, not even one.—Psalm 14:1.

The fool says in his heart, "There is no God." They are corrupt, doing abominable iniquity; there is none who does good. God looks down from heaven on the children of man to see if there are any who understand, who seek after God. They have all fallen away; together they have become corrupt; there is none who does good, not even one.—Psalm 53:1.

4

At Fourteen—Depression and Anger

For wrath kills the foolish man and envy slays the silly one.
—Job 5:2.

I am poured out like water, and all my bones are out of joint;
my heart is like wax; it is melted within my breast;
my strength is dried up like a potsherd, and my tongue
sticks to my jaws; you lay me in the dust of death.
—Psalm 22:14.

The first year was in a blur, a daze where I was making adjustments not at all comfortable or happy at the new environment. Having gone past the first year at RI had not been comforting; I was just one of those massed under the bell of the normal distribution curve. I went to the D class in the second year still trying to understand all that went on and what might lie ahead.

Drawn into the class debating team, I was like an automaton with a self-prepared script that had passed muster—scrutiny and approval—from the team. I felt no great passion for the proposition or opposition of the topics as we ascended through the preliminaries, to the quarter-finals, semi-finals, and the finals. The only person with that appearance of any passion or conviction about the topics was often the last speaker. The earlier three speakers in the team put up the ammunition and the last speaker lighted the fuse and summed it all.

My performance at the band crossed the acceptable line but still relatively mediocre; more was required, no one told me, I simply knew. It became clear I needed help in the area of sight reading and interpretation to which I spent much time humming as I read the score at home; allegro march speeds helped improve instrument output handling and this I acquired through joining an outside band of adults. The efforts culminated in the purposeful development of my appreciation of music and playing skills at the euphonium and trumpet.

English was all about comprehension passages, essay writing, and the un-absorbable ubiquitous grammar. I remembered nothing about grammar. In the very hot sticky afternoon air, where the words of the teacher echoed up the high ceiling, bounced about in a cacophony that in partnership with drowsiness put all things uninteresting to near slumber. The afternoons were a great time to nap had it been permissible. Mathematics was generally all well until I hit a huge wall with simultaneous equations when I understood nothing taught. Perhaps I had not been able to figure out at that time the value of simultaneous equations in its application, if any, to the functioning of life. As in a small enclosed room when the light as suddenly switched off, my panic button went off and I did not *flee* to recess but stayed to *fight*, and finally the binds came off and I saw the light. During that half hour recess, I was determined to just solve all the problems on simultaneous equations in the mathematics textbook and stayed on the task. The purpose of simultaneous equations became redundant, the goal was to understand the method and apply it so as to solve them. *Just do it!* So it was. Purposeless learning . . . can be a dangerously *silent* philosophy in pursuit of the end. Mathematics was to prepare us to know how to reckon, that is to add, subtract, multiply, and divide in the practical transactions of daily living, be it in money matters, or in measuring area or volume. As diligent young children we were all easily pushed to anxiety by the pressures of getting them done right even before understanding what purpose they served, as in putting the cart before the horse. It was all well for the national purpose of growth and development, of moving up the ladder of economic wealth to a higher standard of living, supposedly good for the happiness of the populace in general, for the sense of excellent governance in our political administration, and kept the government in its desired pedestal. *Therefore is my spirit overwhelmed within me; my heart within me is desolate.*—Psalm 143: 4.

Having gone past the first year at RI had not been comforting; I was just one of those massed under the bell of the normal distribution curve. I went to the D class in the second year still trying to understand all that went on and what might lie ahead.

4.1 Unknown Fear

For a short space of time, I had recurring nightmares of falling headlong into a dark bottomless abyss and waking up abruptly, shocked. A distressing emotion had found its way into my soul, as a foreboding of impending peril, horror; an unease caused by real or imagined concern and anxiety. It had a lot to do with a solicitude of not having done adequately well, forcing a self-imposition to rise above the previous performance. Reality had worked its way into my rest, as unfriendly illusions attempted to shaken my soul. It did not last long, they shook off, and preoccupation with the work at hand, the assignments, debating, band practices, and various other activities kept the focus. Still, a fear of the unknown kept me on edge, lest I should slip into difficulty and not recover from it to run the race. When the anchors were less than sure, the waves easily buffet the ship. *Trouble and anguish shall make him afraid; they shall prevail against him, as a king ready to the battle.*—Job 15:24. *Terrors shall make him afraid on every side, and shall drive him to his feet.*—Job 18:11. *Fearfulness and trembling are come upon me, and horror hath overwhelmed me.*—Psalm 55:5.

Endnotes

With God there is no fear, be it known or unknown, be it real or imagined, for He is the Creator, Almighty-Omniscient-Omnipresent, One who watches over us in knowing and loving care. We are His creation, His people. He feels our weakest murmur, our weary faith as we slide to the depths of the valley below. He hears our silent sighs, our soundless cries as we walk through the valley of the shadow of death. His rod and His staff, they comfort us . . . goodness and mercy shall follow us all the days of our lives. We will dwell in the house of the LORD forever. Who is like Him? *The fear of man bringeth a snare: but whoso putteth his trust in the LORD shall be safe.*—Proverbs 29:25.

4.2 Alternative Band—Sousa's marches

Sousa was an American composer and conductor of the late Romantic era, known primarily for American military and patriotic marches. Because of his mastery in marching music, he was 'The March King'. Among his best known marches were The Washington Post, Semper Fidelis (Official March of the United States Marine Corps), and The Stars and Stripes Forever (National March of the United States of America). Other marches included Liberty Bell, El Capitan, and The Thunderer. He also developed the sousaphone much like a tuba, coiled around the player's body with the huge bell rising above the player.

To master Sousa's marching music, one had to have the sense of his style, his composition, and for a bandsman one had to be proficient in playing the instruments that featured in them. Those on trumpets, bass, sousaphone, trombones, most of the brass instruments, and the percussion had the opportunity to stand out in his music. The wind instruments particularly the piccolos could let their high-pitched running notes float in the air and rise above all when on the field. The glockenspiel like a portable metallic keyboard provided the same effects as the piccolo. For someone in the marching brass band, Sousa's brand of music required proficiency in playing skills along with score interpretation even though the music kind of carried the player along.

I learnt many of Sousa's music when I joined the St. John's Ambulance Band (SJAB) outside of school on Sunday afternoons; it was a personal extra-curricular activity. A neighbourhood friend who was trying to improve on his drumming skills joined SJAB before I did. We bumped into each other one day and we picked up the discussion another time, he checked with the SJAB and they decided to look me over. They auditioned me on a Sunday and decided they could use a baritone/euphonium player. They had use of a classroom at the old River Valley High School along River Valley Road, and the musical instruments kept in an adjacent room provided by the school. It was part of the St. John's Ambulance Brigade in Beach Road. SJAB is voluntary and played for any of the Brigade's drill and official ceremonies as well as any affiliated civic service functions. They provided the uniform and instruments; we did not have to pay for anything used and occasionally we collected a small token allowance for the service rendered. The SJAB band players were mostly working adults, some were professional players in night clubs, and Chinese educated. They spoke in Mandarin mostly and occasionally attempted in English when addressing me. We got along fine. The language at hand was music. There were generally two groups of key people at SJAB—the more classical traditional brass band type and the smaller group of modern individualistic *ad lib* type. SJAB played Sousa's marches and modern Japanese as well as Chinese themed pop music. They had interesting expressions that were not like those I played at school. SJAB was an alternative band exposure for me and did my band music much good in improvement and in enrichment. This was such a wonderful opportunity I had; the experience brought a sense and purpose to my music career at RI, through to the Singapore Armed Forces during the latter part of National Service, and culminating in a short career as a French horn instrumentalist at the then newly birthed National Theatre Symphonic Band; I was a pioneer member. *Whatsoever thy hand findeth to do, do it with thy might; for there is no work, nor device, nor knowledge, nor wisdom, in the grave, whither thou goest.*—Ecclesiastes 9:10

Or saith he it altogether for our sakes? For our sakes, no doubt, this is written: that he that ploweth should plow in hope; and that he that thresheth in hope should be partaker of his hope.—1 Corinthians 9:10. . . . *I count not myself to have apprehended: but this one thing I do, forgetting those things which are behind, and reaching forth unto those things which are before, I press toward the mark for the prize of the high calling . . . .*—Philippians 3:13-14.

4.3 Class Debating Team

The team leader, Kumar picked me as one of the debaters for the team. It was a four-member team that included Kwok, and David. Kumar was the gab, held a fitting aquiline nose, fair skinned, and of Indian Malayalam, spoke with a typical Indian accent very clear and pleasantly accentuated, he could go on talking, and no one would attempt to stop him. We all left it to the entry of the teacher for the next lesson. He was unusual in the way he spoke much like an old tough-minded granny trying to tell a younger person about what was wrong or right, very directive and instructive. His vocal range was broad but naturally spoke above the middle register. Kumar would occasionally break into laughter when he realised how silly he looked or sounded when we stared at him as if mockingly. I never quite knew what happened to him except that he left RI and never came back to school in secondary three. News was that he moved with his family to elsewhere in the world. We all enjoyed Kumar's presence; he was simply a different and unique personality that made us laugh. David, another member of the debating team was probably the tallest in class, the dreamer, always in his own world and when called upon to comment, he would stand up not knowing where to begin. With some prompting from the one next to or in front of him, he would attempt to make up comments that made no sense until further questions from the teacher offered him salvation in finding the hook inferentially to the issue at hand, to wiggle out of the difficulty. You might say he was thick-skinned for the many occasions for his inattentiveness, and never showed any sense of being ruffled, never angry or loud, always seeming collected, but truly outside the mainstream. David's vocal range was low to middle. David became an accountant later in life. Kwok was very studious and good looking, fair skinned, wore black-rimmed glasses, always donning a natural smile, an outcome of his configuration. Kwok's interest was in chemistry, all about chemicals and chemical reactions, an influence from his older sibling. With a white trench coat, he looked a perfect scientist, kind of a young Doctor Who. Kwok's vocal range was middle to high. I never knew what became of him. Since I had mentioned the debaters' vocal ranges, mine was simply an untrained narrow middle, with no attempt to challenge the high, nor try the low.

I had no idea why I was included in the debating team, I thought it might have been my clear pronunciation, ability to articulate, and good diction. I was second speaker throughout the competition. Here was a clear opportunity to practise all that I had watched of Perry Mason and the Defenders in arguing cases in court on television. It was a definite exposure at least to public speaking and I wit it not pass me by.

It was jittery standing on the large wooden theatrical stage raised about three feet above the hall's wooden floor. Looking up at the tall microphone stand, I stood as a bare lone figure before the audience, holding a piece of my argument, under dim yellow lights hung sparsely from the unusually high ceilings of the dark cavernous hall, filled with a layer of darkness hovering over every face that sat on the floor. Past the fifth row of students sitting on the floor in front of the stage, I could barely make out the faces shrouded in darkness; I was speaking to a dark blanket of at least twenty more rows of students that appeared as compressed into a sheet of blackness. I was on the stage of closely jointed wood flooring that creaked with bored disapproval at every step and movement. The atmosphere was frighteningly sullen as in facing a full panel of Grim Reapers abhorrent to any plea or argument, with only one purpose of tearing them to shreds. The judges and audience could hear the paper in my hand rattling from the uncontrollable shaking of every bone in my body. I might have fainted but sheer persistence in embarrassment saw me through. I had all the diction, pronunciation, and statements of argument in order; I lacked a sense of presence, too much lost in myself, in my self-consciousness. What was lacking was the necessary training to be fluent in using language effectively, to express persuasively and forcefully beyond myself, to aptly articulate the thoughts and arguments, holding down self-consciousness peeking over my shoulders. I learned from it and improved the next time. Practice hones all the rough edges and takes a lifetime! This is all well, public speaking requires of us occasionally at the most unexpected of times to reveal our true selves in our beliefs and our understanding. Nevertheless, communication with another person or a small group happens almost all the time. You have to be . . . in order to be able. Be ever prepared.

We went clean through the quarterfinals, the semi-finals, and to the finals, and won! The debating competition was a daze to me. I was grateful for the experience to fall on one that who seemed an unintended and most unlikely candidate. Who knows except the One who carefully watches over us in love, who in eternity past has blue printed it? *Let your speech be alway with grace, seasoned with salt, that ye may know how ye ought to answer every man.*—Colossians 4:6.

4.4 PM Lee Kuan Yew's Son

We were having a combined band practice with Catholic High School, whose drum major as pointed out to me was our Prime Minister Lee Kuan Yew's oldest son. He was generally tall, fair-skinned, had an almost shorn head, not bald, closely trimmed; donned black framed glasses, worn all white short-sleeved shirt and long white pants matching the black leather shoes. Endowed with mildly disproportionate large lips that seemed to pop out from the thin face, expressionless, he did not smile throughout, very stern, unimpressive, had an off-normal look about him. He seemed lonely. I wondered what life was like for him to be a Prime Minister's son. He had a drum major's mace. He was a senior, two to three years older. Today, he is our Prime Minister and a great guy far different from my earlier and younger picture of him that was. What a transformation! Did education make it possible? Was brilliance always in the gene? Was accessibility to the means of education necessary to make that brilliance? Was nurture and upbringing the key influence? Not education and nurture alone could cause it. It must be the deep and lasting workings of experiences in life that brought about the change, something that cut home to the heart, deeply, and brought the inside out. Who can know the depths of our soul? Only He knows. For the PM's son, God in His Providence had made him our nation's leader today . . . *that we may lead a quiet and peaceable life in all godliness and honesty.*—1 Timothy 2:2. *A good name is rather to be chosen than great riches, and loving favour rather than silver and gold.*—Proverbs 22:1.

4.5 My Sight—Mathematics

The afternoon sun, poor lighting, heat, fixed blackboard (dark green chalk board), all contributed to poor vision. When one's sight is handicapped, that poorly designed spacious classroom—broken

61

only by intermittent rectangular support columns from floor to high ceiling, where booming voices muffled and resound when sounds simply looking for surfaces to bounce off without consonance to any purposeful structure—causes the mind to drift into drowsiness. The old overworked fans in all its ostentation from times past, whined listlessly overhead, failed to turn down the sweltering afternoon heat. The whole place was as a civilised cave that sounded and reeked of a hostile cavern.

Simultaneous equations were a puzzle. That enigma unravelled through sheer effort not as in a conventional process but through reverse engineering. It was a case of solving problems without an understanding of the purpose of simultaneous equations. Just go with the flow, follow the procedure and one got it made. It was easy after getting it right. Perhaps it was the teaching approach that did not expose the application that made mathematics a subject of endless formulae and equations.

Mr. PH, our mathematics teacher was also head of the National Cadet Corps. He was rather short of stature, loud-mouthed, yet unable to fully open his mouth whenever he spoke as though he had some precious thing in it that would drop out if he opened it a little more. He sounded like he had been shouting much of his life, intimidating by the manner he spoke as though he was commanding a platoon of cadets, totally inappropriate in a civic classroom; he smoked not in class but outside the building. He wore small glasses and moved his head and eyes as though he was long-sighted which I did not believe he was. He had a drooping tummy held by his shallow pants aided by a narrow belt. One incident that completely took me by surprise, even left me in shock was when he slapped Vij my classmate. Vij was a big body of flab and when Mr. PH slapped him on the left cheek, he literally lifted off his ground. Had I been in Vij's place, I would have gone flying some ten paces. The whole class watched this episode with much horror and one could sense all breathing stopped for a few moments as a deep hush ran through the room. We understood how badly it hurt Vij as he had his hand over his cheek as he returned to his seat. Even though Vij was an easy going person, I suspect this incident could have an enduring effect somewhere or sometime in his life.

Teaching as expressed in ancient languages means 'to throw', 'to cast as an arrow or lot'. It is also used as of thrusting the hand forth to point out or show clearly. The concept then of education is therefore that the teacher puts forth ideas and facts to the students as in the sower casts seeds into the ground. Teaching is not a methodical and external but rather is internal and affective to the learner's understanding, growth and development. I am thankful there is no longer such abuse and violence in the classroom. Perhaps, Mr. PH's behaviour may be called a disrespectable transgression, while other respectable transgressions may still lurk in the background.

I made up my mind then and there to speak to Pa about my pair of glasses. At all cost I must not have anything to do with Mr. PH other than listen to his lesson, get my schoolwork done, see well, and move on. I abhorred him, the very sight of him.

Endnotes

An incident like that above of Mr. PH slapping a student was unbelievable for me particularly by a teacher who was representative of the time-honoured profession of teaching. How can one teach others to learn when the very action that proceeded from the educator was contrary to all good faith of moulding and building strong characters for the future of society? If such egregious conduct were to happen today, it would be in the press the next day. The social media would get buzzing all over the country and perhaps outside our borders. The school would reprimand the teacher and possibly dismiss him. The parents of the student assaulted would bring criminal charges against the teacher.

Social norms and expectations offer a general deterrent to transgression; the law serves a stronger specific deterrent, but love the essence in teaching serves as an unconstrained guaranteed embrace of care and civility, and needed no deterrent.

We attend school to receive instruction, to be taught, to acquire knowledge, to be illuminated in the knowledge taught and acquired. Often we need the teacher in his approved pedagogy to expose the subjects to us and elucidate the concepts/ ideas taught so that we can complete our understanding at the level taught before passing upwards to receive 'strong meat'. *For when for the time ye ought to be teachers, ye have need that one teach you again which be the first principles of the oracles of God; and are become such as have need of milk, and not of strong meat. For every one that useth milk is unskilful in the word of righteousness: for he is a babe. But strong meat belongeth to them that are of full age, even those who by reason of use have their senses exercised to discern both good and evil.*—Hebrews 5:12-14.

4.6 My Goggles

My eyesight turned worse under poor lighting in the classroom and glare from the afternoon sun, added with Mr. PH's violent personality to which I was abhorrent, I decided to talk to Pa about the glasses.

The problem with having glasses was that one had to be accustomed to them and that took a while. They were unlike a pair of good eyes attached to one's body and never fell out when knocked. Glasses created problems, and one had to constantly be aware of their vulnerability. A momentary absence of mind was disastrous. When I played basketball before school or during the recess, while jostling for the ball, a careless hand easily swiped off my glasses. I had to immediately abandon play and tried to recover my glasses. Many things could happen: a lens cracked, or the nose bridge support fell off, the ear arms bent, screws holding the ear arm loosened, etc. I learnt to come up with temporary solutions that used Scotch tapes, rubber bands, glue, and strings as temporary 'band-aids' until more permanent solutions were available. Where the damage was mild, it was liveable. Where it was breakage I had to take them to the optician to size up the damage and the attendant cost. When things were bad and unsalvageable, I had no choice but to let Pa know that I needed a pair of glasses.

Our eyes need caring, and together with our ears, they are literally the receptors of external data and information by reading or hearing or a combination of both to help us perceive, recognise and discern physically. Our brain lends that cognitive property to assimilate and process the information received by those faculties. Having less than effective receptors can end up with imprecise information feed and lead to its faulty processing, resulting in incorrect conclusions and bad decisions. *But, as it is written, "What no eye has seen, nor ear heard, nor the heart of man imagined, what God has prepared for those who love him".*—1 Corinthians 2:9.

4.7 Oh! What Grammar

Grammar was frightening only because it made absolutely no sense to me. Learning grammar was like holding the bolts and nuts of language to tie down the ideas in communication; of agreement and concord, of a verb and a noun or of subject-verb-object, understanding subject and predicate, style, structure, patterns of usage, and so on with the belief the student can and will consciously apply them. For me grammar naturally happened in the spontaneity of communication. Grammar was like the laws of nature, one cannot hope a ball to stay up in the air and not come back down to earth for the law of gravity defies it. Something sounds odd in 'he run like the wind' instead of 'he runs like the wind'. Grammar was like breathing and needed not teaching. It was the same with marching, when the left leg was out the right hand simply moved out, there was an innate synchrony. Try marching with left leg and left hand moving out at the same time, we would be out of tandem and look terribly weird, terribly unnatural. I do hope you have not picked out a grammatical error thus far, and if you did, my theory is dead unless we can track it to the editor's remiss. Grammar is to writing or language as air is to breathing. It was confounding to have to learn it. Yet English grammar is as English law that governs communication in the English language. For the language to be effective as a vehicle of thought in the road of communication, grammar is as the Rule or

Law to hedge it to be articulated comprehensively and coherently. *The natural person does not accept the things of the Spirit of God, for they are folly to him, and he is not able to understand them because they are spiritually discerned. The spiritual person judges all things, but is himself to be judged by no one.*—1 Corinthians 2:14-15.

4.8 Streaming: Arts or Science

Streaming was dependent on results at the final examinations held at the end of secondary two. One got to enter the science stream in secondary three, and these included good results in English, mathematics, and science. I had no idea what it was about or what it meant. Hearsay was that science guaranteed a future. Arts students were the ones with poorer grades. These were what unsupported suppositions sounded like. In looking back, it was generally natural for arts students to have poorer grades in science subjects, and probably vice versa. Opinions were that no future vested with the Chinese language; one must focus therefore on English. We needed more science graduates for the future; we needed engineers to build our industrial base and capability: investors were more willing to set up shop in Singapore. Do not waste your time with literature, history, and all things arty and 'farty', a callous application of flatus to aimless, foolish pursuits that served no real economic purpose. The world of the future was about science and engineering—the cornerstone of the nation's economy.

When my own children were growing, entry into the Science stream offered more options due the wider range of faculties to choose from, and more degrees offered by the universities. The combinations of subjects reckoned into wider permutations for doing a course of study at university albeit not necessarily in the field desired. The goal was to graduate with a bachelor's degree. However, as it turned my daughter disliked Mathematics but suffered in diligent study to ensure she kept a straight-A's academic score sheet. My son hated

Mathematics for its 'uselessness' and decided on a consistent score of UG (ungraded) for the subject. Eventually they were all in the Humanities. At the end of the matter, there must be a problem with the combination along with the attendant streaming. Where could time be better applied? It is so scarce.

Hmmm . . . that was the bowl then: get in line, and pick up the alphabets (B.Sc., B.Ed., B.Acc, B.A.) in the alphabet soup. The alphabets were good only where we now are, in our lifetime. Collecting too many of these strings of alphabets weighed one down too quickly to do more. Not having them made one less fit for this professional world. I would exchange them all for the experiences in faithfulness and trusting in His Providence. *For who hath known the mind of the Lord, that he may instruct him? But we have the mind of Christ.*—1 Corinthians 2:16.

5

At Fifteen — Hanging On, Hope and Acceptance

I am poured out like water, and all my bones are out of joint:
my heart is like wax; it is melted in the midst of my bowels.
—Psalm 22:14
But he that shall endure unto the end, the same shall be saved.
—Matthew 24:13

*T*he spirit of a man will sustain his infirmity, but a wounded spirit who can bear. Deep depression of the spirit is one of the most grievous of conditions one can experience: denial of the truth becomes an escape, grievances surface to excuse the situation, anger stirs the spirit to bemoan injustice, helplessness melts the heart to give way to despair, and confidence dissipates strength to offer only flimsy strands of hope. Two years at RI was a listless, humbling, sobering, and steadying experience; it was like having made a dash through the fire singed, scalded somewhat but not too badly, like running the gauntlet emerging with cuts only skin-deep, no threatening debilitating gashes, just enough to understand pain, where it hurts worst, and what to do to avoid it. A sense of hope descended upon my life, offering a light lift in spirits, an encouraging nudge to move forward. Up until now, it was about *walking after* all that presented itself letting them lead the way. I was now beginning to feel ready to *walk before* all that came on, taking charge and leading the way. Will better days lie ahead? Forerunners have been there, travellers have made that stretch of the journey. To each his own and they have emerged alive for better or worse.

Up until now, it was about walking after all that presented itself letting them lead the way. I was now beginning to feel ready to walk before all that came on, taking charge and leading the way. Will better days lie ahead?

5.1 First Trumpet and 'jazz'

The trumpet eluded for a little over two years when all that remained was the euphonium, a little bulky for my size and stature. The mouthpiece was nearly as large as my mouth and I initially thought I was going to puff out my life on it. We learned that we do not blow as air through the mouthpiece; we buzzed or created a buzz that sustained an even flow of vibrations that ran through the straights and bends of the tubes. The mechanics not clear to me then was about creating the buzz and building the air column in the tube, the buzzing of the lips determined the frequency, hence the pitch, and with the cooperation of valves channelling air through the tubes produced different notes of the musical octave. The trumpet was supposedly more difficult because of the smaller mouthpiece, the range of playing from the middle to the higher registers, the buzzing more intense. Generally, its size matched by physical stature, its mouthpiece made sense with my lips, playing at first trumpet complements my early aspirations in music. It was something I was happy at playing, the demands on the first trumpet clearly called for more intensive effort in terms of technique, accuracy, musically-fitting sound without appearing forced, blending well with other instruments in the band, precise phrasing, and a sound sense of rhythm. There was a need to listen to different styles of music, exploring the range or register of the instrument relative to the music scores we usually played. I realised a definite need for wider exposure through listening on radio, as printed scores were not readily available beyond what we had at the band library. I listened regularly to classical, big band, and jazz on the radio or borrowed audio cassettes. Cassettes were unfriendly when one wished to rewind or fast forward to a particular segment. That was the age of sequential access. In the last two decades, random access had been the norm. It was like the music records of those times where one needed to place the reading needle on the track of the desired song/ music.

When I was 'found out' and offered a place in the first trumpet section or the lead trumpet section, that—called the tune, highlighted accents in the score—it was a complete vindication of my early disappointments and all the extra effort outside of school to prepare for a remote possibility of ever playing first trumpet. What mattered was the process of getting there—the desire, the effort of serious practice for hours on end, the extra time on Sunday afternoons at the St, John's Ambulance Brigade Band still playing the baritone much like the euphonium—more specifically to improve on speed reading/ playing, expression; ability improved much from proficiency at John Sousa's brand of marches. I became very good at memorising all my marching scores so that when out in the field the coordination of playing well, marching in formation became naturally smooth, one thing less to worry about. The memory work was not really memory work; Sousa's marches were wonderfully sensible and ringed/rhymed within me as they dovetailed into my person. When walking to take a bus, when showering, whenever finding time in between school and home activities, I would 'da-da-da' the tunes, visualising the notes and the fingerings on my trumpet. It was not quite an obsession just a balanced intensity; I was beginning to love and enjoy my music and my playing.

Jazz originated from the Negro communities in America's Deep South and was a mix of African and European music traditions, with much use of blue notes, improvisation, syncopation, slide notes, and polyrhythms. Syncopation was the style that caught my whim; there was a lilt, a sense of anticipation that came naturally as though it was part of music, and it put life into the music. Late in secondary three, I managed to scour about the music shops and found a book with music scores of Dixieland music, more specifically 'Blues'. It was the only remaining copy, a little brown and old. I bought it at a bargain and it served me very well in developing an interest in such music that required development of certain skills and sense to it.

At the end of the matter, I was rewarded the first trumpet position but what truly mattered was not the *bigger task*; my *capacity for the bigger responsibility*, for the bigger task was the thing that counted most. *He becometh poor that dealeth with a slack hand: but the hand of the diligent maketh rich.*—Proverbs 10:4.

I am the first trumpeter from the left

I played French horn for the National Theatre
Symphonic Band in the pioneer batch

5.2 Additional Maths—The One Real Teacher

Mr Ho was my Additional Mathematics teacher. He talked loudly with a slight drawl as if to stress his point. I collected a F9 for the subject in the second term examinations. 'F' stood for 'fail' and '9' was the lowest grade score. My position in class put me at the end of the pack. How did that happened? I knew the answer to that question. Mr Ho knew it too. There was nothing to hide, it was not poor teaching on his part; it was not that I was retarded and unable to understand differential and integral calculus: I was completely delinquent during his lessons, never attentive, always at some frivolous activity like talking in whispers, joking, and tickling away. I deserved the score. It woke me. Mr. Ho was not to let me off the hook. He announced to the class my poor score and told me in front of the class that he would watch me like a hawk, and he did just that. Was I embarrassed? I did not feel embarrassed. Why should I? The result was a deserving one. We reap what we sow: nothing more, nothing less. My job was to get back on the right track and Mr Ho's was to make sure I kept my attention on his teaching. Whenever I was inattentive during lessons, he would break a piece of chalk from the one he held in his hand and threw it hard at me, to remind me or for me to pick up the chalk and go to the black board to write out the answer to a question. At year's end, I was rewarded with a P1, essentially a grade 'A'. Mr. Ho was a dedicated teacher, fearless, full of understanding how boys of our age tended to drift, and the best methods to harness that energy to the right places. His method was publicly dress me down and to persistently interfered my distractions with chalk throwing, seemingly a boyish prank of sorts. Once I was under control, all other subjects, and life itself came under a common rethinking. My position rose to fifth in class. I went on to the best science class in secondary four. I was truly grateful how this second half in secondary three changed my sense of focus and got me back on my feet for the crucial or landmark secondary four. *As a bird that wandereth from her nest, so is a man that wandereth from his place.—*Proverbs 27:8. *Thou hast also given me the shield of thy salvation: and thy right hand hath holden me up, and thy gentleness hath made me great. Thou hast enlarged my steps under me, that my feet did not slip.—*Psalm 18:35-37

5.3 Zhu taken—Go be a Doctor

I ran down to help carry Zhu out of uncle's pick-up truck, while mum picked some of Zhu's paraphernalia. I was 15 years old. We were expecting her return home for a short, more like a brief stay. This was one of those things Pa and Mie never shared with us in terms of the background to Zhu's homecoming, planned as a news 'blackout'. They might have information we never would learn about. They were simply tight-lipped and went about in a manner that involved us without ever causing us to have a need or be curious to ask. It was like in Robert Frost's two-lined poem:

We dance round in a ring and suppose,
But the Secret sits in the middle and knows.

Zhu went to Woodbridge Hospital a place for mental patients. She had trouble at the half-day school for the mentally disabled and could not continue there. Being at home was a hazard for her: she would break the lock and roamed the streets.

Pa and Mie went to work,
Siblings kept a watch on her:
Behind walls and bushes we hid
Perchance the neighbourhood kids
Thoughtlessly taunted and teased.

They jeered at her for their childish pleasure.
They insulted her for being lesser of a human.
They scorned her for being weaker of mental defence.
We appeared from hiding to chase them away,
We warned against further provocation.

She was simply retarded and not deserving of Woodbridge, but there was no other place. Zhu was physically strong and when manhandled she would fight herself out of it. Apparently, at some point during her stay at Woodbridge she had a tiff with the attendants there and accidentally scalded by boiling water. Getting word from the hospital, Mie sought the use of uncle and his pick-up truck to fetch Zhu home for a few days. I carried Zhu up from the pick-up truck; it was a picture beyond belief, unthinkable-unthinkable, and downright inhuman. Completely emaciated, knees all bent as though locked in place, uttering meaningless broken streams of sounds—moans apparently, and blankly looking at me, wanting to say something yet beyond her strength. I was someone she knew. I wanted to address her, say something to comfort . . . not a word came. I had no sensible offer of solace. Painful as it was, we could only show our unchanged love for her by ensuring no further deterioration of her immediate physical wreck already very much beyond palliation. Any mental anguish she might have been through at that time was beyond us. Communication with her remained walled by her condition, by our shock, and by our loss of any human sensibility—it was past feeling, it was just grief, grief of silence. Zhu was now on the sad extreme of what she once was: strong, loving, bubbly, wanting always to be in on the action. She was now so light, so very light; no muscle mass, no spring in her skin, looking much as dried bean curd skin wrapped about the bones. Physically shrunken, reduced to helplessness, she now was worse than the Jewish race awaiting their ignominious and inhuman deaths in Hitler's concentration camps—all energy drained from her soul, what remaining strength left was for her to draw her fleeting and receding breaths.

When we got up to the house, Mie asked me to put Zhu down on the long wooden sofa and to find a belt from Pa's wardrobe. We put the belt around her waist and tied it to the sofa, Mie explained that Zhu must not suffer any falls as her bones were brittle, any broken bones could seriously deteriorate her condition, and restraint was appropriate. For much of the day she would utter sounds that we were unable to decipher and could only draw near in sympathy. Empathy was beyond us, she was not normal like us; we could not get under her skin. Throughout the day, her weak utterances—moans or groans—found us in difficulty comprehending.

After a few days with us, Mie sent her back to Woodbridge. Within a week, the hospital informed Mie that Zhu had died from bronchia-pneumonia. Mie went to pick her body from the hospital. She arranged a simple, a little more than a pauper's funeral for Zhu, no ceremonies, nothing. Pa and Mie could not send off the hearse according to Chinese customary rites, Mie kept us out of any participation—the undertakers quietly took care of it.

Unheralded, she came to us,
Misplaced, you might think.
Displaced, she was not.
Purposeful, I can vouch.
Shared halting moments of joy,
Anxious moments of concern,
Living legacy of love, and
In a hush, she left . . . and was not.

An unheralded birth . . . that did not fit in with the world . . . fitted in with us as family . . . to a despondent end . . . but purposefully; joy and anxiety overwhelmed in her love passed on to us . . . quietly she was passing through.

And the LORD God formed man of the dust of the ground, and breathed into his nostrils the breath of life; and man became a living soul.—Gen 2:7. So man lieth down, and riseth not: till the heavens be no more, they shall not awake, nor be raised out of their sleep. O that thou wouldest hide me in the grave, that thou wouldest keep me secret, until thy wrath be past, that thou wouldest appoint me a set time, and remember me!—Job 14:12-13.

I made up my mind to aim for entry to pre-Medical; a rash decision indeed.

5.4 Meeting Shakespeare, Animal Farm, and To Kill a Mockingbird

It was in secondary three that we learned about William Shakespeare for the first time. The play we studied was *Twelfth Night*. It was categorised as a *comedy* and it was. At that time, I saw the play as just a lot of nonsense over nothing, with the love-sick egoistic Duke Orsino brooding over the beautiful Olivia, yet liking his handsome page-boy Cesario, who was actually a woman by the name of Viola. Viola was trapped between not telling Orsino that she loved him because she was in disguise as a page-boy, and telling Olivia that she could not accept her love her because she Viola was a woman. The English in the play was of the Elizabethan era, crafted for the stage, and the style made it easy to learn. There was a 'singing' flow about it and good for recall. I scored for this subject, much of the analysis was not due to my brilliance; I mastered them from the notes in the Minerva guides that proliferated the Indian bookstores at Bras Basah. I read them and found them useful, reasonably sound, and they came from lecturers who were familiar with the past years' examinations on this particular play. In secondary four, we studied Julius Caesar classified as *tragedy*, also by Shakespeare. This time I was really good at many things Shakespearean as I had begun to appreciate his work, I easily memorised the whole play. Perhaps 'memorised' was not the right word, it was more akin to having a sense of Shakespeare's style of writing, and picking up the flow was like breathing. When asked to provide critical analysis of the motives and intents of characters in the play, or of the general import of the play, I was able to quote passages accurately within it to enter a studied and clear exposition of them. In that year, we also studied George Orwell's Animal Farm and together with the secondary three book, To Kill a Mockingbird by Harper Lee, English Literature as a subject opened my mind to the powerful ideas resident in these books and plays about human nature, about Communism/ totalitarianism, about racial injustice to black people in America's Deep South. The writers depicted those ideas in stories that powerfully reveal the language, the culture, and the prevailing 'mind' at that time. I found myself locked into them, carried away by the worldviews and problems of the day. Literature exposed to Lenin, Trotsky, Stalin, communism, the USSR, not in a deep manner but enough to offer the necessary backdrop to our study of Animal Farm.

All of the above exposure to socio-political issues was coincidental to my receipt of other free journalistic materials such as *The Plain Truth, Newsweek,* and *Time.* I breathed and lived in all that had happened and reported, as my daily bread; my engagement in them was intense to the point of being overwhelmed. [Bible]

5.5 The Plain Truth

The Plain Truth, a magazine of Understanding was a Christian magazine whose publisher was Herbert W. Armstrong head of the Worldwide Church of God (WCG). They ran the Ambassador College, to provide education for their members and would-be members. I actually signed up for a free correspondence course simply out of curiosity. There was a high content of Christianity in the course and a lot about prophecy that were completely outside my interest. There was no way I would even start on the program. I bade it farewell and let the materials go down the rubbish chute. The Plain Truth also released several little booklets mostly about beliefs and practices, and one that I remembered well was the Seven Laws of Success. These laws were commonsense in nature except for the seventh, which was a belief in God! How could I? I was a Buddhist, though a shaky one by that time; bred to abhor God, Christ, the Bible, and all things Christian. I had worked on the other six laws but this seventh was definitively outside my purview and worldview.

Years later, after I came to know of Christ I learned that the broad Christian community considered Armstrong's brand of Christianity a cult, a movement that deviated from mainstream unorthodox Christianity. For a long time now, I no longer receive The Plain Truth. Some years ago, out of curiosity, I learned that several groups have splintered off and the largest was the United Church of God (UCG) from whom I continued to receive the print edition of *The Good News* carrying the same subtitle of The Magazine of Understanding as it was in the Plain Truth, and *Vertical Thought* targeted at today's youth. Today, I also receive a daily e-mail Bible devotional/study called *The Berean* from Church of the Great God (CGG) the group that continued Armstrong's brand with a slightly different focus, and can now surely understand the differences in the splintered groups, a case of being in the *light* from the time I was in *darkness*.

For me, The Plain Truth was an economic-socio-political reporter of the times and selling the future (Kingdom of God) to which it was linked. Nonetheless, its former reporting role impressed me hugely and engaged me quite completely; its religious role was totally oblivious to me as I selectively left them outside my reading. I was the natural man attracted only to the natural world. Even Buddhism my professed faith, was to me very much in the natural realm. Karma in my mind never attained to the spiritual for its lack of substantive evidence and persuasion. It was merely a man-made theory.

Had I been a Christian then and had allowed the overwhelming issues of the day to grip my *understanding* I could mishandle Biblical interpretation. Cults are such, brought about by mixing doctrine with worldly matters without weighing them in God's balance: His Word. The devil in his world of darkness, in the name of humanity, lies to man that God does not care, that God is incapable of setting right all the wrongs of this world. Man fails to consider God; seeks his own limited understanding, looks to his own self-centred opinions, considers self-pleasing preferences, makes unquestioned suppositions, and intoxicates from the mixing of carnal with spiritual, of evil with good, of the corruptible with the incorruptible, of darkness with light, of the temporal with the eternal. The definitive black and the conclusive white now become acceptable shades of grey.

For many shall come in my name, saying, I am Christ; and shall deceive many.—Matthew 24:5. *And many false prophets shall rise, and shall deceive many.*—Matthew 24:11. *All scripture is given by inspiration of God, and is profitable for doctrine, for reproof, for correction, for instruction in righteousness: That the man of God may be perfect, throughly furnished unto all good works.*—2 Timothy 3:16-17.

5.6 Large Vocabulary

Every word new to me, from a book or from *The Plain Truth, Newsweek,* or *Time,* I wrote it down in my 200-page exercise book, organised in alphabetical order. My vocabulary grew commendably large that in later years, a friend nicknamed me 'the walking dictionary'. Having a large and strong vocabulary allowed me devour almost any book without needing to check the dictionary and therefore not truncate the flow of knowledge acquisition and thought; regular reviews over time improved recalls, just as constant application reinforced understanding. More importantly, a comprehensively large vocabulary ensured I had at hand a powerful tool to communicate my feelings, emotions, thoughts, and ideas effectively. It allowed an articulation and eloquence that carried over to the one who reads as intelligent and true. Application required writing practice in order for the vocabulary to become useful. Regular recall of the vocabulary was necessary to remember them well, to this end there was little trouble as whenever I had time in between study, class lessons, on the bus when going to school I reviewed my handwritten 'dictionary'.

Regular doses of the Word Power section of Reader's Digest had been instrumental to spurring me on to acquisition of a rich volume of vocabulary. It was as a quiz with answers located in another page, providing a kind of test that constantly stirred me on to attempt to beat it.

Incidentally, I have carried with me a paperback called *A Dictionary of Synonyms and Antonyms* by Joseph Devlin. Published in August 1961, it was a prize I won in a Singapore Buddhist Youth Organisation Vesak day essay writing competition. It had been a close companion whenever I write in my earlier days. Sometimes a word I used did not quite so perfectly express the thought I intended; this dictionary helped me look up the synonyms to nail down the more precise word. If the synonyms did not help, I could think of the antonyms and worked into the synonyms of the antonyms. I usually found the word I was looking for. It is now rather brown-looking, still in healthy condition but very usable and portable; all these years I had wrapped it in plastic which had now become crisped and tore at the edges where folded to hold on to the book cover. Today, I do not carry it around with me; it is just my desk copy more like an overworked old friend retiring contentedly on my desk having run the race with me. I now use the internet for my dictionary and thesaurus in line with the age and times. *Whatsoever thy hand findeth to do, do it with thy might; for there is no work, nor device, nor knowledge, nor wisdom, in the grave, whither thou goest.*—Ecclesiastes 9:10.

5.7 Found Again

In the second half of the third year at RI, I found a certain peaceable rhythm in life. As a kingdom in ruin, and presently restored through a tour de force of an indisputable strong man wanting changes in place to afford order amidst the chaos, to allow peace to take root, the proper administration and control of all flash points, purging of problem elements, institution of the rule of law, and relentless pursuit to that end. I was not that strong man. That strong man was hope, a sense of hopefulness, a convergence of reality and hope. Meaningfulness floods every rivulet, every stream, and every brook that once lay parched, as in a sultry desert land, despondent, resigned to barrenness.

Restored from a lost state was undeniably a great joy as in holding the reins of ten horses with incomprehensible measure of strength, confidence, and control, of knowing in a surge that the elements have collaborated, filled with an assurance of their unquestionable cooperation.

Endnotes
Was I lost before? I certainly thought so now. It was not as though all things worked against me. However, as the Chinese saying goes,

". . . the one in the midst of it is lost; the one standing beside is clear." I was lost. Loss of the natural man is just a temporal one, he can look for or a replacement of that which was lost. That which was found or replaced can again be lost. For the spiritual man when he has God's Spirit in him walks in the light, he cannot be lost unless he chooses to return to walking in darkness. *What man of you, having an hundred sheep, if he lose one of them, doth not leave the ninety and nine in the wilderness, and go after that which is lost, until he find it? And when he hath found it, he layeth it on his shoulders, rejoicing. And when he cometh home, he calleth together his friends and neighbours, saying unto them, Rejoice with me; for I have found my sheep which was lost. I say unto you, that likewise joy shall be in heaven over one sinner that repenteth, more than over ninety and nine just persons, which need no repentance.*—Luke 15:4-7. God is foreseeing. He knows. He directs. He decides. He wills.

5.8 Varied Interests

In secondary three, there were several classmates who had been interesting for their individuality, interests, and involvement.

KC who sat next to me, with whom I shared many jokes that kept me inattentive in class, and received a resultant failed score in Additional Mathematics in the second term. He had a cheek dimple when he smiled, rather playful. KC was a member of the 2102 RI Scouts Troop and showed the many knots he learned as part of the scouts training. He had to progress from tenderfoot through to different levels of competency. KC was generally good at water/poster-colour painting and had been particularly good with a technique he learnt from his brother on painting trees so that from a distant there was a three-dimensional sense in the light and dark shades created from a range of green colours applied by dotting or 'blobbing'. KC was Cantonese and was easy-going, not easily ruffled, not too bothered about academic achievements, happy with his slightly better than mediocre results. He was a generally contented person that I was happy to have for a friend.

Soh was a rugby player, small-mouthed, tended to smile often, bringing out his high cheeks, his speech always scattered with chuckles and Mandarin, a very natural person with no airs about him. He had a mild myopia and it did not affect his rugby when he had to take off his glasses. In fact his small black framed glasses sitting on his high cheeks made him look unique. Occasionally he came into class with an arm cast in plaster, a neck brace, a hand bandage from injuries in rugby. He once came in with a single crutch for a leg injury. Rugby was certainly a rough sport. He was slightly short and had an odd gait as though he was bow-legged. Soh was a tough fellow physically but open and real, tells secret rugby jokes that you would not hear about here. Soh continued into the Science stream but had no clue what happened to him after secondary four.

Sim had a crunch on women teachers and had a tendency of sharing his private comments with me as I sat in front of him, and probably a safe person with whom to share them. Sim received a scholarship to study Medicine in Australia three years later during which time he wrote back about the rather corrupted seamy campus life there. I often bantered with him about my concerns for his women patients should he graduate. We lost touch with each other and I have absolutely no news of his whereabouts. Sim played basketball for RI, very tricky, quick, agile, and he fitted the game perfectly as he had few qualms about trickery, devious or otherwise. His family was upwards of the middle class and dealt in drapery. He wore a wrist watch with metal clip-on wrist chain that he habitually toyed with. Sim had perfect eyesight. He was not academically well placed in two and a half years at RI, always in the end classes and picked up only in secondary three. After that he was on track all the way. Something had tweaked. I never what it was. We enjoyed each other's company generally, I more than he.

"I the LORD search the heart and test the mind, to give every man according to his ways, according to the fruit of his deeds."—Jeremiah 17:10.

6

At Sixteen — Re-building, the World is Big

Who shall separate us from the love of Christ?
Shall tribulation, or distress, or persecution, or
famine, or nakedness, or danger, or sword?
—Romans 8:35

Say, "Thus says the Lord GOD: Will it thrive?
Will he not pull up its roots and cut off its fruit, so that it
withers, so that all its fresh sprouting leaves wither?
It will not take a strong arm or many
people to pull it from its roots."
—Ezekiel 17:9.

I continued to read The Plain Truth magazine and renewed my free subscription whenever I received a request to do so. The magazine had a certain focus in playing up and highlighting an age of discontinuity in world affairs. The social malaise of the times, the wars that went on, détente and stand-offs, global economic storms and crises, European history in the midst of inconceivable developments within the Common Market, the emergence of the EEC, shifting politics that threw the world in disarray, and a new world order of sorts, and religious decline as the magazine saw it. It revealed a disillusioned society in the United States unsettled by the Vietnam entanglement, the ensuing domestic protests, the proliferation of drugs and crime, blacks and racial segregation. It was the age of the *hippie* culture, and a sort of break-with-the-norm cultural revolution.

> . . . an age of discontinuity in world affairs. The social malaise of the times, the wars that went on, detente and stand-offs, global economic storms and crises, European history in the midst of inconceivable developments within the Common Market, the emergence of the EEC, shifting politics that threw the world in disarray, and a new world order of sorts, and religious decline as the magazine saw it. It revealed a disillusioned society . . .

Readers' Digest was second hand, bought at a real bargain at the pasar malam (night bazaar). They were months and years behind, all well for us as the articles were seldom time-sensitive; they were more inspirational stories and had a pull-out book section. I love their 'word power', quotable quotes, and jokes. Had they been time-sensitive, Time, Newsweek, and The Plain Truth covered them more than adequately.

With the TV news coverage and the local Sunday Times (for we could only afford a Sunday copy and forego the daily ones) were more than enough to whet our appetites for all that was going on in the world. All the entertainment was no longer as valuable as information. The deluge of news in an age of social, economic, and political upheavals caused us to be selective in our consumption of the media. Time was scarce: there was overwhelmingly much to bite off and to chew, to digest, to assimilate, and to be involved. We wanted so much to be a part of the action.

6.1 Chinese and Chinese Teacher

Our Chinese teacher was a fresh graduate from Nanyang University, very dainty, wore glasses, smiling always, sincere and wanting to do a great job at the premier school, and to make a huge impression. The first day of her duty found her very well-dressed in a one-suit light floral dress that ran a lower knee-high spreading skirt, not gaudy. She wore quite matching compatible white shoes with medium-high heels. She looked poised and confident, sweetly smiling, and very pretty. Her session with did not turn out well; the class snubbed her more out of its hopelessness at the Chinese language after three years of absolute neglect. Most of her class talked away, totally ignoring her efforts, they held up the opened Chinese textbook on the desk and held another physics, or chemistry, or mathematics, or literature book right behind the Chinese textbook, hiding them from her view. She attempted to keep up her brave demeanour throughout the lesson. She ended her session by trying to sum it up, hope against hope to secure a last cry of pulling the deserters together, and manifest some semblance of meaning to the lesson, all to no avail as her voice trailed off with a sense of despair. On the second day, she made further efforts to regain the class' attention. It failed once again and this time in the middle of the lesson, she pulled out a tissue paper to wipe off her tears, raising her glasses to do so, her face blushed, not with guilt but with shame of failure. We sensed her sniffing some, the class was pretty heartless and inattentive. At the end of the lesson, she could not much smile; no pretence to hide her despair attempted, no brave front, simply downcast. A few of us got together after the lesson, and decided we would shift to sit at the front row and give her complete attention from the next lesson. There was in our hearts a simple decency, that of gentlemen in the making, to embark on what we did to come to the aid of a lady in distress; nothing more nothing less. The next day it all went according to plan and she was happy and shared much about the words and the history behind the readings for that day. She was thoroughly thrilled with the handful of us who showed willingness and desire to learn at her feet, rendering her the full attention every teacher would love to draw to herself. A leader must have willing followers; a teacher must have inquiring students. There was much to learn and at that time, I often wished we had that sort of fresh knowledge from her approach in teaching the culturally and historically fraught Chinese language. I got a credit for it, a few in the class passed and a large number not too unhappy about failure when they did superbly well in most of the other subjects. Chinese was dispensable as a general view.

We must honour our teachers, be attentive. Always seize the opportunity to learn, to acquire knowledge, and to receive instruction in wisdom, discerning the truth, illuminating our understanding, walking in the light and not in darkness. *And thou mourn at the last, when thy flesh and thy body are consumed, and say, How have I hated instruction, and my heart despised reproof; and have not obeyed the voice of my teachers, nor inclined mine ear to them that instructed me!*—Proverbs 5:11-13.

Teachers need to be patient when they teach their younger learners. Teachers do not aggregate knowledge and simply transfer on to students as processed products. Real learning can only come to us from genuine teaching by teachers who go the extra mile to enhance the learning of that taught. Teaching is instruction; discipline as a condition necessarily follows it, for teaching seeks to inform the taught, to aggregate the body of learning, to illuminate the concepts/ideas, to elucidate the knowledge imparted, and to inspire in its use. *Hear counsel, and receive instruction, that thou mayest be wise in thy latter end.*—Proverbs 19:20. *And they that be wise shall shine as the brightness of the firmament; and they that turn many to righteousness as the stars for ever and ever.*—Daniel 12:3.

6.2 Time and Newsweek

Time and Newsweek magazine came to me with regularity every fortnight from Mie's American employer, Mr. Osteen. He was an oil executive with a U. S. based oil business with interests in the Asia-Pacific region. They came a week or two late after Mr. Osteen had read them. Mie was always on the lookout for them for our benefit. She had permission from Mrs Osteen to remove them for our use. It was no matter we read them late; just having the opportunity to read them was a huge bonus. We had never read or seen such information-packed magazines. Even The Plain Truth that we received monthly could not match these magazines. It was like a week's news in the U.S. and around the world compacted into an easy-to-carry-about magazine format. The styles of language usage were slightly different from the English we learned and applied; some spellings were different too. Exposure to the content in these magazines had been highly influential in engaging my life to realities in the world. They might have instigated some of my views then when one was still wet behind the ears; one's affections were as red hot steel hammered out, and as the clay still wet in the potter's hands, malleable and pliable for use, for moulding. *Counsel is mine, and sound wisdom: I am understanding; I have strength. By me kings reign, and princes decree justice. By me princes rule, and nobles, even all the judges of the earth.*—Proverbs 8:14-16. *The fear of the LORD is the beginning of wisdom: and the knowledge of the holy is understanding.*—Proverbs 9:10.

Endnotes

We are what we read. What we read enters our eyes, works on our brains, assimilated into our hearts and minds, formulating our theories, and beating out our philosophies and beliefs. What we read becomes what and how we think. Had we not have a sound foundational basis to direct the external bombardment of what we read, we could be misdirected. A clear view of who we are, why we believe in what we believe, serve as defence to any external corrupt and adverse influences. The unexplainable concept of *karma* died a long while ago. Our Buddhist foundation offered the good living basis to keep within its hedge. However, it could not liberate us from the bondage of sin. Good clean outward living has no basis to justify us in the face of a perfect and holy God. We are eternally bound to outer darkness until we can have one among us who in obedience to God is willing to lay down *His life*, and who is perfectly blameless to meet God's demand, so that our belief in the saving significance of *His death* becomes our justification.

We think we read for knowledge but in these magazines; we find them as facts through accurate reporting yet spluttered with opinions, with emotional displays in using extreme examples and suggestive photos of ground scenes that goes beyond accurate reporting. Knowledge is an apprehension of facts or truths according to their nature; it conjoins the affection and will. It certainly rules out opinions. Knowledge has greater certainty. The mind is constantly desirous of possessing and increasing knowledge. The highest knowledge that man should seek is the knowledge of God. *Canst thou by searching find out God? Canst thou find out the Almighty unto perfection? It is as high as heaven; what canst thou do? Deeper than hell; what canst thou know? The measure thereof is longer than the earth, and broader than the sea.*—Job 11:7-9. God is knowable in as much as He has revealed Himself to us in nature in creation. *Because that which may be known of God is manifest in them; for God hath shewed it unto them. For the invisible things of him from the creation of the world are clearly seen, being understood by the things that are made, even his eternal power and Godhead; so that they are without excuse.*—Romans 1:19-20. God's knowledge is absolute, unerring, and perfect, complete, all embracing in time and space, and knows the innermost thoughts of the heart.

At the end of the matter, with all the reading and awareness at the age of discovery we are very much spectators: frozen to inaction, helpless, uncertainly hopeful; our abilities inconsequent in the gargantuan challenges, our inexperience in the hands of Father Time and our strength unknown as it was un-tempered. Wherewith is knowledge? Wherefore is wisdom? We become observers, armchair critics, our knowledge un-processed, comes down to us second-hand; wisdom un-distilled, sullied with commonplace views, opinions, conventions that reeks of popular acceptance and the appearance of being knowledgeable.

6.3 English and Literature—A New Voice

The many issues of life—social, economic, political—together with snippets of history engaged my thoughts a great deal at that time. The one place my voice found ground to express was in my essay writing as I was not the public speaking sort. The teacher seldom discussed these issues in class. I wrote private essays unknown to anyone else. However, they could also appear in test papers, and that happened at the G.C.E Ordinary Levels English examination. It was about a social issue that I could not resist taking on and wrote freely and profusely exceeding the booklet of writing paper issued, whereupon I requested for extra sheets of paper. I was so take up by the endeavour that when the invigilator announced that we had half an hour left to complete our work, I realised I had gone overboard and needed to wrap up the writing. However, to do so meant a reorganisation for coherence requiring the removal of several pages of completed writing. To pass the paper, the obvious had to be undertaken, painful as it was. An examination was a test of one's capability in limited coherent presentation of the subject and not of an unrestrained exuberance of ideas, thoughts, and convictions on it. I passed the paper by the skin of my teeth. A lesson learnt was to wisely put our passions under the lid whenever required and to focus on the matter at hand. *There was a time for everything . . .* I was clearly in youthful exuberance and unthinking folly.

A Shakespearean play like Julius Caesar with the plots, intrigues, and study of human nature and their dilemmas was fertile material to structure and organise the issues of life. Without true experience, appreciation was limited only to a supposed cause-and-effect within the time and space of the play. It was canned, a creation by the playwright to depict, to portray human dynamics from a slice of assumed history. At this age of discovery, I saw much in terms of the 'given' that was on the platter but very little beyond, of the truth. Our literature teacher, Mr. Dee loved reading the play out loud as though he was playing several characters and gesticulating with his hand actions . . . a one-man playhouse. He could have done very well if only he could memorise the play while vocalising the characters and having two hands free instead of one hand holding the textbook. His physical configuration, a slight paunch from age, drooping bulldog cheeks, and weak voice, seemed to let the voice run ahead of his utterance all in a split second and trying to pull it back. One heard his voice and saw his mouth moved. A good way of explaining it would be the lightning before the thunder. Light first, then the sound. I have never quite figured out how it worked for him.

In George Orwell's *Animal Farm*, we learned of satire and its use in the exposition and derision of the Stalinist totalitarian ideology. The reversals of 'four legs good, two legs bad' to 'two legs good, four legs bad' highlighted the corruption of ideals in the face of adaptation to worldly reality. One could read further into the exposition, and allowed strong emotions about truth, justice, fairness, and ideals to conjure the evidences of blatant lies, suppression, failures, and dark forces through the acts of man from his heart that is *deceitful . . . and desperately wicked*. Orwell's satire was truly a masterful craft in powerfully moving his thoughts of a political ideology in the context of the recent history of his times and portraying it in a parody with animals. Is there no hope for man? Has he only wickedness and deceitfulness to show, generation after generation? Ah! Can he not rise above the grosser traits that seemed to dog him throughout history? *My son, beware of anything beyond these. Of making many books there is no end, and much study is a weariness of the flesh. The end of the matter; all has been heard. Fear God and keep his commandments, for this is the whole duty of man. For God will bring every deed into judgment, with every secret thing, whether good or evil.*—Ecclesiastes 12:12-14.

6.4 On the Tracks

Life took a turn, rather settled with the direction sufficiently clear to be in focus. For the first time since my entry to RI, I felt life was going to be on the tracks and that a smooth ride begun to manifest. There was a sense of hope that all was well as long as the locomotive was well oiled, adequately fuelled, and kept a steady run barring any obstacles hitting the tracks. I have begun to love most though not all of the subjects in the science stream, particularly English and Literature. They offered me in the age of discovery, an outlet for expression, for finding my 'voice' in engaging the issues of that time. It was unlike the study of mathematics, chemistry, or physics where one studied and presented that body of knowledge learned. All that was empirically visible and measurable, tested and testable, experienced and explainable, belonged to the domain of science and mathematics; English and Literature was about me, about things that were not taught, about my thoughts of them formed from qualitative observation, of recurrences, not so much to seek an explanation for but to make sense of. They offered me an opportunity to rethink, to review, to reconsider and truly understand my deepest feeling for and thoughts of the issues. They gave me a better understanding of my true self—the yearnings, the search for truth that seemed to have deluded me. The heavy shroud of burden of the first three years at RI had all kindly lifted, and there was a sense of freedom. Looking back, *were these the right tracks?* They were rolled on, even if they had not been the right tracks, and our lives have been history on them, have been real, not a delusion. Bearing in mind that *history does not make the man but the man makes history*, I can look forward and imagine only that hope lay ahead. The feeling was similar to Chuck Yeager's breaking the sound barrier, going past the speed of sound (Mach 1) in his test machine, with lots of rattling, fright, and confusion trying to reach the speed of sound. However, once past Mach 1 there was great calm, there was a seeming *alignment* in space and time between man and machine. I watched a full-length black and white dramatised movie on this on television. It can be likened also to *traction* that reduces friction between the tyre and the road surface that they both interact, hence the saying 'the test is when the rubber meets the road'. It was like a yacht catching the wind in its sails, as a long-distance runner riding his *second wind* or *runner's high* when he is exhausted, nearly down and out. Both yacht and runner must be ready, physically equipped for the rigours of wind and sea, of muscles and metabolism.

I was ready for the GCE Ordinary Levels, a landmark examination in our education journey. I was prepared, there was no hesitation, the coast was clear, there was a clarity of all that needed done. I also wanted to join the pre-Medicine class for Zhu's sake even though she had left us. RI had only one class in the school for pre-Med. It was special. Competition was keen from within, and without from students of other top schools. The settlement of the heart held down any turbulence amidst the swirling storms in the 'teacup' or the threatening winds from afar, no longer buffeted about precariously uncertain. *"For we walk by faith, not by sight."*—2 Corinthians 5:7.

6.5 For Zhu: to pre-Medical class

I made it to go pre-Medical. The class is a 2-year program to prepare one to enter the course for Medicine in university with subjects in Biology (and branches in Zoology, Botany), Chemistry (and branches in physical and organic/biochemistry), Physics, Economics, and General Paper (English paper).

The year before when Zhu passed on, I had made up my mind to go to pre-Med and from there on to the study of Medicine to be a doctor. The decision made at a time when there was anguish with the way the medical fraternity handled her placement, and the presumed lack of care and diligence afforded her at the hospital. I knew little about the goings-on as Mie took care of them and kept us siblings out of them. All the anger associated with Zhu's passing was a supposition from presumed cause-and-effect, not a thing we knew or understood at first-hand. I did not understand bronchia-pneumonia until a long time after. I had considered her death caused by the lack of due care at the hospital, by its staff, its facilities, its organisation, and even beyond that: outside of the hospital, the aftercare that never existed in those days. Somehow, the sense was the doctors and hospitals were at fault. The decision to study to be a doctor was something of the moment, as though one could change the way things were or had been. It was simply groundless, a silly bravado aroused by anger, a thing of the moment, absolutely foolish. I had no idea what it meant to be a doctor other than that it was a highly desirable and respected profession. I had not counted the cost and duration, for these would surely bear heavy on Pa's shoulders to support the endeavour. Our financial condition was clear but I yet harboured a false hope based on anger and ignorance. How could one rely on anger and ignorance to ride the swallowing waves of reality? It must surely meet its ridiculous end. The decision was ignorant and ill-conceived caused by emotions that could not take root: it caused no pain, Providence in time put things in their proper places. *For which of you, intending to build a tower, sitteth not down first, and counteth the cost, whether he have sufficient to finish it?*—Luke 14:28

Endnotes

The thoughts of the diligent tend only to plenteousness; but of every one that is hasty only to want.—Proverbs 21:5. *Seest thou a man that is hasty in his words? There is more hope of a fool than of him.*—Proverbs 29:20.

6.6 Religion in certain Declension

Buddhism as a religion of my father had seen a definite decline in my life beyond the duties of rites and rituals, presence at the weekly worship at the Thai temple, observance of the five precepts daily and the ten precepts on special occasions, and attendance and participation on special days and Vesak Day. I clearly had no attachment to the philosophy of Buddhism, no definite commitment to its tenets for dear life; rather, it had become a profession than devotion.

There was no desire to proselytise. There was no mandate at all. There was an absence of a methodology. The culture within the temple had become one of promoting good works, releasing pigeons on Vesak Day, issuing food to the poor, chanting long hours of blessings, fasting, selling presumed power-talismans, and depending on the supposed effectiveness of amulets with no understanding of Buddhism. This had been the heavy influence of the Thai epicurean practices and in no small way propagated by the Thai monks who dispatched from the parent temple in Thailand. Buddhism became synonymous with all things Thai. Monks in the poorer countries go about daily with their food 'urn' to seek alms, walk barefoot for miles in arid rough grounds, to experience poverty, hunger, and contentment in what the day offers. Things have naturally changed.

A defence of the Buddhist philosophy was the natural expectation from someone who when asked for his religion would unhesitatingly state it as 'Buddhism'. On all my official identification documents, Buddhism was my religion. When I was serving National Service in the Armed Forces, engraved on my metallic 'dog' tag (identification tag hung around my neck) was Buddhism to signify my religion in the event I should die or was about to die in training or battle, they would arrange the proper religious rites to respectably and appropriately handle my demise. In fact, Buddhism had little defence required of it, few people bothered to oppose its philosophy; few knew enough about it to do so. It was generally the approach of letting alone be alone. The idea of *karma* alone had many 'holes' in it, many questions about its validity, and about its operation. It taught that every deed, good or bad, must have its result, that 'its fruit must be eaten' here or hereafter. Whoever decides the effect to occur here or hereafter? It was karma. There was no discussion about how and who forgives sins other than hint that we must hopefully do enough good to produce good fruits to overwhelm the bad fruits from our evil deeds. It was like a scale where one attempted to do good to tilt the scale in one's favour, still not quite knowing when these fruits would come on the scale in the here or the hereafter. There was no tracking methodology, just trusting it all to the force of *karma*. Buddhism was a religion easily embraced by the commoner for the reasons discussed as well its affinity with Asian traditions, philosophies, and customs.

There were little available and advanced teaching materials within the Dharma class (Sunday school) to develop one's understanding. A dire lack of qualified and serious teachers; where there was no root, there can be no fruits. At the same time, the temple's library left unmanaged, its stock not replenished, no new additions made, no new interest developed, caused systematic Buddhist doctrine to lose its hold, mingled into and finally sodomised by the pervasive Thai pagan and epicurean culture. I had a little paperback that I won at a Buddhist essay writing competition that served as my resource. Written by a European who had converted to Buddhism, and became a monk, it presented a simple history of how Buddhism came to be, clearly with no intention to substantiate the presentation, rushing quickly into the philosophy or dogma about *karma*—the silent, un-measurable, ubiquitous force that drove the lives of all living things which in turn supports *karma*. I hung on to that book for dear life, it was well-written and contained the fundamentals of Buddhism and yet did not address several nagging questions I had. It was a book written by a believer who was captivated with *karma* and without tearing it apart or turning it inside out, went on to explain it as though it was a real operating model based from his understanding of the concept. It was someone falling in love with another and by some cognitive dissonance raised the object of love on a high pedestal to justify its desirability and worth. It was all fuzzy, too easy to fall for, as though 'good begets good' is such a simple, straightforward common sense concept, that it must be it. It was much too sentimental. The Dharma school was not foundationally-run due to a very small enrolment of students who had little interest at all to learn the tenets of Buddhism. Sound teachers were as few in numbers. The school became a namesake. Attendance dwindled and my interest flagged with it. In the absence of sound teaching and grounding in its doctrine, religion drifted into hearsay. A 'little learning' is proverbially dangerous. *This is an evil among all things that are done under the sun, that there is one event unto all: yea, also the heart of the sons of men is full of evil, and madness is in their heart while they live, and after that they go to the dead. For to him that is joined to all the living there is hope: for a living dog is better than a dead lion. For the living know that they shall die: but the dead know not any thing, neither have they any more a reward; for the memory of them is forgotten. Also their love, and their hatred, and their envy, is now perished; neither have they any more a portion for ever in any thing that is done under the sun.*—Ecclesiastes 9:3-6.

A religion that gave me no inward comfort, no inward rest about who I was, where I came from, and where I was going to; a religion that offered no basis for such comfort, for such rest, cannot be from a perfect almighty true God. My education could not provide that comfort; the socio-political system fails to lend a hand, sport entertains temporally, amusements shams, wealth cannot procure it . . . . *Jesus Christ the same yesterday, and today, and forever. Be not carried about with divers and strange doctrines. For it is a good thing that the heart be established with grace; not with meats, which have not profited them that have been occupied therein.*—Hebrews 13:8-9. *Let us labour therefore to enter into that rest, lest any man fall after the same example of unbelief.*—Hebrews 4:11

Endnotes

Only one way to God the Father—Jesus Christ;
Only one door to the Father—Jesus Christ;
Only one path to inward rest—Jesus Christ;
Come unto me, all ye that labour and are heavy laden, and I will give you rest. Matthew 11:28

6.7 Varied Interests of classmates

For a cursory view of several of my classmates, the following narratives of a selected number of them might offer the reader an insight into student behaviours generally at that time. In all fairness, you may consider this random and unrepresentative, a selection of those about me at that time with whom I had been most in touch.

YH was a big guy, curly-haired, bespectacled, physically well-trimmed, and rugged looking. He represented RI in rugby and judo. Never ostentatious or self-conscious, YH spoke generally in mild tones with occasional sneers hidden in light excited laughter. In short, he appeared to be engaged in listening yet armed already with his own point of view and stone-walled. He had quite an interest in physics and could excitedly talk about the subject as though full of knowledge. YH was nice to have around but not someone you could get close with and be a friend to. He tended to be very transactional in all his dealings with the relationship element far removed. There was a felt distance.

DC had a 'care-less' attitude and clearly manifested his 'live unto me' principle. Very verbose in self-defence of any attacks or snide remarks from others about him, he could shut himself to everything else when he was reading a magazine about planes. He could be loud and uncouth in speech in more trying arguments and disagreements with another; tended to laugh very loudly. He loved planes, and all things to do with planes. Just like a football fan today, he could rattle out the names and history of the plane models, the year of make, the engine-types, the speed, take-off, etc. DC wore a large sporty looking watch about his left wrist. DC had no real friends only social ones.

HY was Hainanese, a clearly rounded in the face and body, loved Mandarin pop songs as a way to improve in his Chinese. He encouraged me to do likewise and showed me several such song books with numerical musical notation, where 1, 2, 3 . . . were the do-re-mi . . . on the English music score. The lyrics went right below each line of musical notes. I looked over them, realised they were rather sentimental, and mostly love songs, quite unsuitable for application to our Chinese study and courteously moved them off my plate. Generally, the language used in the pop songs was contemporary and useful for conversation. HY was good at those pop songs and sitting next to him, he hummed them incessantly while we waited for the teacher. He had the audio cassettes as well and was all ready to loan them to me. I had to turn down the offer for the lack of time and interest in the approach. I did not know what HY did or went to in life after RI.

YG was always talking about politics, mostly coffee-shop type, an influence by his father, a taxi-driver who seemed to have much ground or grass-root exposure from his circle of friends and colleagues. His stance was generally anti-ruling government and the sentiments were of addressing the 'cons' against past and current government policies, seeking to point out past errors, and postulating future outcomes of current policies. He loved political debates and placed himself prominently at every conceivable and available opportunity. For me, he had started to bore like the dripping rain, and usually when he called the class together, I almost was sure what was coming on. YG liked the limelight, not a strong public speaker though a daring and willing one who showed too much in his facial expressions that told more of his mind than his words could catch up on. He was involved with the editorial team of school newspaper. One may categorise him as an activist short of derring-do. YG became a doctor and then later a psychiatrist, and got active in politics for a very brief time, too brief to class a political activist.

KK was a truly humble friend very gentle in nature primarily from having a rather quiet upwards of the middle class family, diligent, and a rather Chinese orientation. His dad was a draftsman. He was Cantonese, grew up in Temple Street in the Chinatown district. He brother was a doctor and he wanted to be one as well. We went to pre-medicine class the following year. He learnt to play the pi'pa, a Chinese lute and kept quite long finger nails that aided in the plucking and strumming of the pi'pa strings. KK though highly proficient in his Chinese, failed his final paper and did a re-take. It was incomprehensible for us and surprised him badly. We went swimming once at the Yan Kit pool when he tried to teach me basic strokes. I did not make attempts to continue for reasons of time, availability of pools near home, cost of travel, entrance fees, and the like. I liked KK a lot; he made a true and loyal friend, authentic in relationship.

SB was Hainanese, used to live on a farm, and was all interested about the eyes, the anatomy, the physiology, etc. his family was upward from the middle class. This interest sprung out of the fact that he had a problem with his eyes; it was a shifting problem and he had not quite nailed down what it actually was. He read quite widely about the eyes, he bought books on them. He was very familiar with eye exercises to improve his vision, he would share his theories with me and as a curious individual, and I was attentive and engaged. Few about us would show enough interest in the subject, they mostly thought it was frivolous. Truly, he had an eye problem to the point of becoming an obsession. At times, he took off his glasses, and at other times, he wore them. SB went on to become a doctor. He was a pleasant, straight forward person, easy, and open.

Endnotes

Classmates were people with whom we cross our paths in schooling life. Some ended up as friends, some as acquaintances with just a little more than just a name or a face. However, the one thing I realised was that they were not people we chose, they cross our paths, and we respond in friendship or in a casual if not transactional relationship—KK and SB from a kindred spirit, while the others were rather casual in nature. In the intercourse, we learnt about people and their natures, their motivations in their behaviours, their characters in the beliefs they hold fast to; those of kindred spirit were small in numbers while the casual or transactional types were significantly larger. Those of the same kind, of kindred spirit had an affinity for each other: in the *natural* world, in common inclinations, in race, language, ethnicity, geography; in the *spiritual* world, only in Christ Jesus, the Son of God, in God Himself.

Think much about what Nebuchadnezzar the most prominent Babylonian king and probably the greatest conqueror in all of history has this to say about God. He was in Bible prophecy of old times. He was in God's plan. He was a natural man, having experienced God's power, and still unbelieving until deeply touched by God. *At the end of the days I, Nebuchadnezzar, lifted my eyes to heaven, and my reason returned to me, and I blessed the Most High, and praised and honoured him who lives forever, for his dominion is an everlasting dominion, and his kingdom endures from generation to generation; all the inhabitants of the earth are accounted as nothing, and he does according to his will among the host of heaven and among the inhabitants of the earth; and none can stay his hand or say to him, "What have you done?" At the same time my reason returned to me, and for the glory of my kingdom, my majesty and splendour returned to me. My counsellors and my lords sought me, and I was established in my kingdom, and still more greatness was added to me. Now I, Nebuchadnezzar, praise and extol and honour the King of heaven, for all his works are right and his ways are just; and those who walk in pride he is able to humble.*—Daniel 4:34-37.

EPILOGUE

Better is the end of a thing than the beginning thereof:
And the patient in spirit is better than the proud in spirit.
Be not hasty in thy spirit to be angry:
For anger resteth in the bosom of fools.
Say not thou, "What is the cause that the
former days were better than these?"
For thou dost not enquire wisely concerning this.
—Ecclesiastes 7:8

Although my house be not so with God;
Yet he hath made with me an everlasting covenant,
Ordered in all things, and sure:
For this is all my salvation,
And all my desire,
Although he make it not to grow.
—2 Samuel 23:5

The age of innocence in the first book led us to the second book, Age of Discovery. We have moved from life being a big bundle of little *light* things to a big bundle of little and *not so light* things . . . At a young age, we do not clearly have a set of beliefs; grounded in them, proved them, and trusted them for our conduct and walk in life. As we got older, life can be quite unchanged and remained as in childhood, unless we think and reflect about our own beliefs, check our understanding, test them, try them and prove them.

Our lives, appointed by God's wise Providence may experience the drudgery, loneliness, and discipline of the difficult life as to the glory and responsibility of having the best possible education. Rest well in those moments of seeming chaos when things do not appear to be in order, when things do not seem to grow and bloom, when there seems a cloud of gloom hanging over our lives. All that happens to us is in His plan for us: the most laborious situations and experiences crafted to try and test our perseverance to become nobler, stronger people. Tarry a little, seek His face, and trust in His will. He has a covenant with us for to fulfil, a covenant that is sure and sealed in blood, in the blood of our Lord and Saviour Jesus Christ.

Faithfulness in undertaking and performing the many duties is our portion in life. We may conduct them without any shining brilliance, nor with great success, nor with notoriety that attracts the world's notice, but with the regular, quiet, consistent, and careful performance as of the trivial and common; faithfulness in that which is least is the greatest in God's sight. In every piece of honest work, however irksome, laborious, and commonplace, we are willing workers for God. We must trust Him for our daily need not necessarily via a direct handout. He will cause growth of the corn, but man must harvest, thresh, grind out the flour, knead the dough, bake, and distribute the bread. God uses man in myriad ways to provide the means that serve His ends in His merciful care of His children.

Faithfulness in undertaking and performing the many duties is our portion in life. We may conduct them without any shining brilliance, nor with great success, nor with notoriety that attracts the world's notice, but with the regular, quiet, consistent, and careful performance as of the trivial and common; faithfulness in that which is least is the greatest in God's sight.

We may go through the times and seasons appointed, but *better is the end of a thing than the beginning thereof: and the patient in spirit is better than the proud in spirit.*—Ecclesiastes 7:8.

We each have experienced diverse situations in life, through the physical or the emotional circumstances in which we grow and develop. People are born into many races, many nations, many classes, people who are big or small, tall or short, dark or fair, rich or poor, intelligent or less so—they all exist and gather in this world—doing their own things, living their own lives. God looks at the world of people as strictly two types, groups, or categories: the Wheat or Chaff, and no shades of grey between them.

I know thy works,
That thou art neither cold nor hot:
I would thou wert cold or hot.
So then because thou art lukewarm,
And neither cold nor hot,
I will spue thee out of my mouth.
—Revelation 3:16.

The Wheat believes in the Lord Jesus Christ, led by the Holy Spirit, sees himself as an utter sinner, and flees for refuge to the salvation offered in the gospel. The Wheat loves Jesus, lives unto Him, and serves the Lord. The Chaff has no saving faith in Christ, no sanctification of the Spirit, no cleansing out. The Chaff practises formal religion on the outside and is not inwardly regenerated. The Chaff is fake, not convicted, hence non-committal and superficial, only a professor never a practitioner. *Behold, I have refined thee, but not with silver; I have chosen thee in the furnace of affliction.*—Isaiah 48:10

Times in the age of discovery are overwhelming ones; times of darkness are not times of judgment. They are times of providential opportunities to tarry, to listen, and to understand the '*what*' of those times and not the '*why*', for 'why' is in itself a judgment of Providence, a proud demand for answers that are the prerogative only of the Creator. Consideration of 'what' breeds a realisation of our helplessness, our inability to comprehend all that has befallen us, our complete lowliness and humility for which He would be kind and merciful to render us succour in those overwhelming times. The 'what' further informs of an attitude that claims no rightful privileges before our Creator except those that He graciously proffers, without any faltering doubt, they are free, and unconditional . . . *the way of man is not in himself: it is not in man that walketh to direct his steps.*—Jeremiah 10:23. *Nay but, O man, who art thou that replies against God? Shall the thing formed say to him that formed it, "why hast thou made me thus?"*—Romans 9:20.

Do we not see God's nature: His holiness? The reflex of His holiness requires Him to exact justice so that His nature is not violated, not compromised. Holiness is the absolute standard of God. Disobedience to God is sin, contrary to His holiness. Justice is required. Sinful man is blemished, born in sin, continues in sin, and unable of himself to satisfy God's holiness for reconciliation to Him. Man has need for help from one who has God's nature; from one who lives as man yet is perfect, blameless, and without blemish. Such a one can stand before God to advocate an acceptable justification on account of which He is—the Son of God. He lived a blameless life on this earth as man for only a man can stand in place of another man to advocate for him—the Son of Man; for what He accomplished at the cross—as perfect substitution for man, undeniably corrupted and completely depraved. There can be no reconciliation, no justification except through the Son of God, Jesus Christ. *Draw nigh to God, and he will draw nigh to you. Cleanse your hands, ye sinners; and purify your hearts, ye double minded.*—James 4:8. *Then shalt thou call, and the LORD shall answer; thou shalt cry, and he shall say, Here I am. If thou take away from the midst of thee the yoke, the putting forth of the finger, and speaking vanity . . .*—Isaiah 58:9.

The many little things in life had moved from ease and joy in *innocence*, entered into a phase of *discovery* that awareness and knowledge bring with it the attendant understanding and vexations; a maturing and growing process of engagement that must necessarily come to pass. Knowledge grows in us in time, from study, from experience, from application to the things we do, the thoughts we think about, and the manner by which we conduct life. *For every one that useth milk is unskilful in the word of righteousness: for he is a babe. But strong meat belongeth to them that are of full age, even those who by reason of use have their senses exercised to discern both good and evil.*—Hebrews 5:14.

Two things have I required of thee, deny me them not before I die:
Remove far from me vanity and lies:
Give me neither poverty nor riches;
Feed me with food convenient for me:
Lest I be full, and deny thee, and say,
Who is the LORD?
Or lest I be poor, and steal, and take the name of my God in vain.
—Proverbs 30:7-9.

At the end of the matter, we all start out travelling the same road. Some of us take a turn at the next twin fork, some continue on. On we trudge, till we come to a place of multiple forks, smaller numbers still take the straight road. At every turn of life, we face decisions, decisions that test our character inside of us versus the things the world offer. What is that character? It is faithfulness to the duty at hand, shutting out the allures outside, torn between ease and the difficult. Faithfulness works out that character. That faithfulness requires courage to boldly face the task, take it on, and pursue that duty to its completion, to its end, no wavering, and no melting of resolve. The will cannot be laid save in faithfulness. Not talents, or brilliance, or abilities, or sheer genius will make faithfulness stay its course. It is not in the things we do, few or many, but in how we undertake and do them. Did we give of our best? Did we stretch ourselves to give of the best? Did we give it from deep within us? Did we offer all we have? The day is never done . . . the race not run when duty is left to linger . . . undone.

At the end of the Age of Discovery there was a sense that I had kept faith with all that was my portion in life: experience as He meted out, talents He had placed in my bosom, sinful tendencies for which He had corrected, early or first lessons in keeping a holy life of a natural man to reveal their hopelessness. I was not in His garden. I was a *bruised reed* outside His hedge for I walked in darkness; His righteousness could not consider a *broken reed.* He nursed the bruised reed to life, extended His hedge around it, protected and cared for it. His love and mercy could not *quench* the *smoking flax;* He fanned it to burn, added flax, and raised the flagging dying smoke to life. Now . . . I walk in the Light. I know my beginning! I know the Way, the Truth, and the Light!

I have kept to the straight road to scorn the many delights dangled towards the road forks and ignore the many sweet sirens that tug at the heart. Though still a heathen then, the Lord was faithful and patient for He knows when the clay shall be ready to yield to His Will, for His glory. He had His eye on the clay from the very beginning. Be faithful. Walk straight at where the sun rises. Pitch your tents there. Watch for it to rise. You will see the light for His love and His embrace is overwhelming. *His lord said unto him, Well done, thou good and faithful servant: thou hast been faithful over a few things, I will make thee ruler over many things: enter thou into the joy of thy lord.*—Matthew 25:21.

A NOTE TO READERS

———◆◆◆———

For readers who have enjoyed this first book of mine, Age of Innocence, as well as this second book, AGE OF DISCOVERY, you may wish to look out for the next book, Age of Restlessness in your local bookstores or the regular online retailers. It will be available in the few months.

Any comments, suggestions, and communication you wish to have with the author may be directed to: BlessedpRobin@gmail. com

ACKNOWLEDGEMENTS

I owe all to my Creator, who made all things; *and without him was not anything made that was made*. I was as a *bruised reed* and as *smoking flax*, yet He drew me unto Himself.

My Creator had given me Pa and Mie who have been excellent parents despite their limitations, which they overcame through simple, wise, practical means, centred in love. They were also my 'teachers' in life. The subject they specialised in was 'LOVE'. Most distinctive was their love through their 'walk'. They once walked in darkness; by God's grace, they walked in the light. As accomplished saints, they have passed on into glory.

Special Thanks I owe to my brothers and sisters in Christ at Shalom who share a love for God and His ways, persevering ever to deepen their understanding of and obedience to Him. These are people I am completely at ease and at home with, free from earthly agendas, always watching out for each other, extending their hands, their means, their homes, and their lives in fellowship.

Thanks also belong to Trafford Publishing for being a part of my virtual team in this second book, as I had learnt the relevant and the much through its effective system. Sydney Felicio is my right arm in this partnership, ever responsive.

Thanks I must extend to Chris Lodovice from the Author Learning Centre (ALC) who regularly serviced and offered assistance whenever and wherever possible.

Thanks can only silently pass to all those who have been a part of my life, now as in the past, a list of which is much too long to produce here. Many have gone to their own places, and many others still alive may never know about the existence of this book.

Heartfelt Thanks rightly rest with all who have read the first book, Age of Innocence. You have shown friendly interest and that alone is warm encouragement in a reader-less world that is slowly becoming. Many have shared open, supportive, useful, and usable verbal feedback; a selection of the written ones had gone into the book as endorsements with permission.

ABOUT THE AUTHOR

───◆◆◆───

R obin is semi-retired and is an executive coach/consultant. Accounting trained, he now practices as a financial services consultant in the area of life, trusts, and estate planning. He is married, with two adult children, a son-in-law, a granddaughter, and a grandson, and lives in Singapore. He worships at a Bible-believing church. Robin writes under a pen name.

Robin believes that life is not accidental but has a purposeful design privy only to the Creator. He catches glimpses of it as he reflects on his own life. Time reveals a coherence of all of life's *past* events as he sees them dovetailed or integrated into the ultimate divine purpose.

This book *Age of Discovery* is the second of a planned sequel that seeks to understand a *concept* of life by reflecting on events and experiences wherefrom in logical stages of development, and revealing the completed part of the divine blueprint as he sees it. The first book was *Age of Innocence* published at the end of 2012. A third book, *Age of Restlessness*, offers insight into Robin's life between age 17 and 21, is expected to hit the bookstores about July 2013. The last book in the sequel, *Age of Brooding*, takes us through his life from age 22 to 26 before he married and raised a family, should be available at book stores in October 2013.